CREATING A HOME
DESIGNING AND PLANNING
BEDROOMS

WARD LOCK

CONTENTS

5	Introduction
7	Planning your bedroom
9	Storage in the master bedroom
15	Bedroom lighting
19	Bedroom furniture
23	Dressing tables
27	Attic bedrooms
33	Room for a guest
39	Highlighting the bed
45	Three stages to a perfect bedroom
51	Nurseries: newborn to two
57	Toddlers' rooms and play areas
63	Children's rooms: five to twelve
69	Teenagers' rooms: 12 to 17 years
75	A young person's bedsitting room
81	Finding space for a parent
85	Beds: mattresses and bases
87	Different types of bed
89	Choosing bedding
91	Wardrobes
93	Bedroom furniture
95	Index/Photographic credits

© Ward Lock Limited, 1988
Artillery House, Artillery Row, London SW1P 1RT, a Cassell Company

Based on *Creating a Home,*
First Edition © Eaglemoss Publications Limited, 1986

ISBN 0 7063 6728 6

Printed in Great Britain by Cooper Clegg Limited

INTRODUCTION

In the small homes of today, bedrooms need careful planning to be more than just a place to sleep. Storage, leisure pursuits and study must be catered for as well, and working out how to achieve all these aims, especially on a limited budget, is a complex task.

Designing and Planning Bedrooms is full of colour photographs showing bedrooms of every conceivable style, to suit every member of the family: from the new baby to grandma. Starting with a chapter on basic planning – where to position the bed, how much storage space to allow, where to install lighting – progressing to the most difficult part: planning an efficient storage system for clothes and other items in the master bedroom, whether it is the popular built-in type, or consists of individual cupboards and shelves.

At the end of the book there is a buyers' guide illustrating the different kinds of beds, bedding and bedroom furniture on the market. Lighting also has a chapter to itself as it plays such a major role in a multi-purpose bedroom.

Also featured are a variety of specialized bedrooms: ones designed to exploit the awkward shapes of an attic; guest bedrooms; nurseries; children's and teenagers' rooms; and bedsits for both young and old. Another useful chapter shows how to build up your ideal master bedroom in easy, affordable stages.

Designing and Planning Bedrooms is full of inspiration for anyone who dreams of the perfect bedroom but doesn't quite know how to achieve it.

PLANNING YOUR BEDROOM

Your bedroom may not be on public view but it still merits care and attention to detail.

Good bedroom planning helps make the most of what is often a smallish space; clever storage simplifies your daily routine. And an eye for decorative possibilities helps to create a stylish, welcoming room.

Which room For some people, the bedroom is just a place to sleep. Others like a retreat where they can relax, read, listen to music or watch TV. In some homes, the bedroom may be the only area for quiet activities such as sewing, studying or writing letters.

The first step in planning a bedroom is to choose the most suitable room. Most houses are designed with the bedrooms near the bathroom and away from the living area, but if the existing layout does not work for you, there is usually an alternative. If you like to sleep late, for example, avoid a room which overlooks the street or gets the full glare of the morning sun. If you just want somewhere to lay your head for eight hours, opting for the largest bedroom would be a waste of space. It might be more sensible to give children the biggest bedroom, equipping it with toy storage and desk space, thus easing the pressure on the rest of the house.

Fitted or furnished The layout of your bedroom depends essentially on how you tackle the problem of storage. Fitted or built-in cupboards decrease usable floor area but can be tailored exactly to your requirements. Traditional storage furniture, such as a chest of drawers, wardrobe, blanket box and dressing table, can create awkward dead spaces, but are often attractive in their own right.

Bedroom space
Far left: 75cm is needed around a bed for changing sheets, circulation and vacuuming, fit castors if the bed is against a wall. Slightly less space will do between two single beds.
Left: the minimum allowances around and between two people sharing a double bed and around one person in a single bed.

MAKING A PLAN
Start by drawing a diagram of the room on graph paper, marking on all existing features, such as windows, doors, alcoves, radiators and cupboards. Include the position of all services, such as telephone or TV aerial points, electric sockets and switches. Then, working to the same scale, draw the shapes of the furniture you own or intend to buy on a separate piece of paper, cut them out and arrange the pieces on the room plan to find the best arrangement.

Bedrooms are not subject to heavy traffic but access is still an important consideration. Beds should have enough clearance to allow for circulation and changing sheets. If space is tight, fit castors to the bed to make it easier to move. Make sure there is enough room for cupboard or wardrobe doors to open fully, that drawers pull out without obstruction and that there is a clear route between the bed and the door.

Note any aspects that could be changed to increase space or practicality. You might want to rehang a door to improve access, move a radiator or add a new electric socket or switch.

LIGHTING
Work out the lighting you need on your room plan. General overhead lighting is flexible if controlled by a dimmer switch, preferably operated by the door *and* the bed.

In addition to general lighting, you probably need some task lights. Direct lighting from a table lamp or spotlight is essential for a study or hobby area. Fit a light inside a deep wardrobe with a small switch in the door jamb (rather like a fridge door).

Mirror lighting A dressing table mirror illuminated by a pair of tall candlestick lamps or a row of Hollywood-style bulbs to either side, as shown on the right, casts an even, shadowless light across the face which is ideal for putting on make-up.

For a full-length mirror, an overhead bulb casting enough light to illuminate you from head to toe without shadow is ideal, especially if you are dressing for artificial light; daylight-balanced fluorescent strips either side of the mirror give a closer reflection of true daylight.

Bedside lighting A bedside lamp should be adjustable, so that it casts a direct beam on to your book without shining into your eyes. In a double bedroom it is best to have two bedside lamps, so that one person can read in well-directed light if the other wants to sleep.

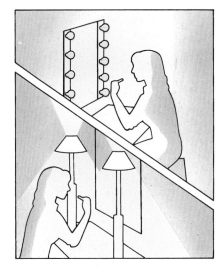

STORAGE SOLUTIONS

Although bedrooms tend to be small, the demands for storage are often high. If you don't want to disappear under a pile of clutter, every inch will have to count.

Start by making a detailed, specific list of what you need to store:
- winter and summer clothes
- evening clothes
- outdoor wear
- suitcases and handbags
- bedlinen and blankets
- laundry
- shoes and hats
- cosmetics and jewellery
- books
- sports or exercise equipment
- items relating to specific activities, such as a sewing machine.

Once you have made your list, see if you can find a home for some of the items elsewhere. Suitcases, for instance, could go in the loft; bedlinen in an airing cupboard; the laundry basket in the bathroom. Winter clothes could be packed away during the summer months and vice versa. Consider fitting a box room or part of a hallway with cupboards and shelves to take the overflow.

Whether you are planning to have built-in or free-standing furniture, there are many space-saving ideas.
- Hang ties, belts and beads in a row over a rail fixed to the back of wardrobe or cupboard doors.
- Store shoes, tights and socks in tiered wire baskets or pocketed shoe tidies.
- Blankets and linen could go into an ottoman at the foot of the bed or in pull-out drawers underneath.
- A laminate countertop could serve both as a work surface and dressing table.
- Fit a second rail halfway up a wardrobe or cupboard to double the hanging space for jackets, skirts and shirts.
- Extend built-in cupboards right up to the ceiling to make full use of the wall area.
- Fit roller blinds to cover shelving or cupboards and save the space needed for door clearance.
- Use a shop rail for hanging clothes if there isn't enough room for a wardrobe or cupboard – but keep clothes in bags to protect against dust and fading.

Above all, don't skimp on space. Allow room for expansion – don't jam your wardrobe so full of clothes that dressing becomes a chore. A cupboard should cater for specific needs: evening dresses are 45-50cm longer than standard daytime dresses; and small items get lost in deep drawers.

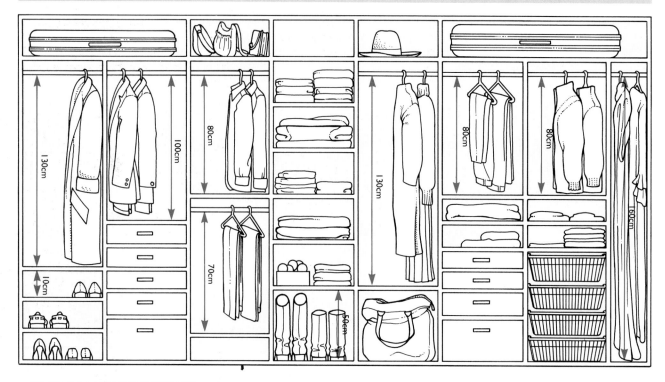

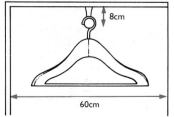

WARDROBE PLANNING

People vary in size. So, obviously, do their clothes. The dimensions given above are for an average adult man and woman sharing a wardrobe.

The overall height of the cupboard can vary according to the height of the room. The depth should be about 60cm, enough to accommodate a bulky coat on a large hanger. The main hanging rail should be slightly above eye level, at about 180cm, allowing clearance above of 6cm to hook and unhook hangers. Clothes are heavy, so long hanging rails must be supported from above by strong brackets.

BEDROOM STYLE

Bedrooms are where you begin and end the day, so they should be decorated and furnished to provide a peaceful, comfortable atmosphere that will set you off on the right foot.

To create a general feeling of calm, avoid too bright, insistent colour schemes and busy patterns. Keep it simple with light, pastel shades and small patterns. Increase the feeling of space by co-ordinating patterns and colours for bedlinen, curtains or blinds, and wall finishes. Mirrors are also useful, maximizing natural light and giving an illusion of depth.

Don't neglect the personal touch. An armchair, or even a sofa if there is enough room, will promote a feeling of comfort. Fresh flowers and decorative objects provide accents of colour.

STORAGE IN THE MASTER BEDROOM

No matter how tidy you are, an efficient storage system will transform your bedroom.

Whatever its size, a master bedroom should be a calm haven from the hectic activities of the rest of the house. But if it's strewn with clothes, shoes, magazines, jewellery, sports gear, make-up and all the other bits and bobs that seem to have no home, it will never feel like a peaceful retreat.

The way to create a feeling of space *and* ensure that all the personal clutter that lives in the bedroom is safely out of sight is to give yourself sufficient, well-planned storage. With careful planning, you might even find you have room for a TV, so you can watch the programme of your choice for a change – a real luxury.

FOCUS ON FURNITURE

Make your bedroom furniture work for you. If, after deciding where to put your bed and dressing table, you are left with one clear wall, uninterrupted by a door or window, you will be able to have a range of floor-to-ceiling wardrobes built in along the entire length of the wall – and enough storage space for clothes and shoes, and possibly for the rest of your possessions.

Free-standing wardrobes and chests give you less storage space than built-in ones but, if you are considering moving fairly soon, this may be a more sensible option.

Roomy chests of drawers, beds with drawer divan bases and bedside tables that incorporate small cupboards all provide vital extra storage space.

A low chest or trunk at the foot of the bed provides extra storage without taking up a lot of space.

Make the most of every inch of space inside wardrobes. It is unlikely you will need an entire run of full-length hanging space, so consider adding a low rail in one section for shirts and racks for storing shoes. And incorporate drawers, open shelves, or wire trays – perhaps even a linen basket – into the cupboards. Store suitcases and seasonal or holiday clothes which are not often needed in overhead cupboards.

Classical elegance

Built-in wardrobes look less overwhelming when the line is broken with a bed or dressing table. Here off-white double wardrobes with a period feel are topped by a row of high cupboards, creating an alcove for the bed. The built-in headboard has a shelf along the top for lamps and books, and for displaying photographs and ornaments. A matching dressing table and drawer unit gives storage space for smaller items.

SPACE AT A PREMIUM

In a small bedroom, storage space is at a premium – and so is floor space. The best solution is one that looks good, works well and gives you room to relax.

Before committing yourself to new furniture, work out a budget. There's no point in spending a fortune on getting every last detail perfect in an elaborate fitted wardrobe if you plan to move in a couple of years. Remember that improvements like these may not necessarily always add their full value of your property.

Whatever type of furniture you choose, plan it carefully so that you end up with the best combination of hanging and shelf space.

Equally important is to make sure that the style of storage is in keeping with the character of the room itself. Think about the design, finish and colour, not forgetting final touches such as knobs and handles that can affect the whole look.

In an older building, the room may still have many of its original features. If the picture rail and ceiling mouldings are in good condition, it would be a pity to cover them with fitted cupboards. Of course, you may have to, in which case, matching up the lines of these features with the wardrobe doors will help to preserve the room's character.

Bedroom storage isn't just about wardrobes, of course. There may be odd corners that can be used for extra drawers or shelves.

The space underneath the bed is often wasted – consider a drawer divan base, or a free-standing drawer unit that slides under for packing away winter blankets or summer clothes that would take up precious space in a wardrobe.

Free-standing This is the most flexible option. It is a positive advantage to be able to move things around if you feel like a change. And, of course, you can always take it all with you when you move. The disadvantage is that free-standing furniture tends to take up more room than built-in cupboards.

With free-standing furniture, make sure you give the room a sense of unity. Choose second-hand pieces made of the same type of wood, for example, or items from one of the many ranges of modern bedroom storage units that are designed to mix and match.

If you find yourself with a rather

unrelated mixture of pieces, painting them all the same colour will help to achieve a unified look.

Built-in For a really neat look that maximizes storage space while taking up minimum room, it's hard to beat built-in, wall-to-wall wardrobes.

Ranging from simple shelf and rail arrangements to versatile modular units and very sophisticated systems of shelves, drawers, hanging rails and compartments, fitted wardrobes come in a wide variety of styles.

There are many off-the-peg systems available, or doors and rails can be bought from a DIY supplier, ready to fit yourself. Alternatively, you could get a carpenter to build in the wardrobes for you – this is a particularly good solution for an awkward-shaped room.

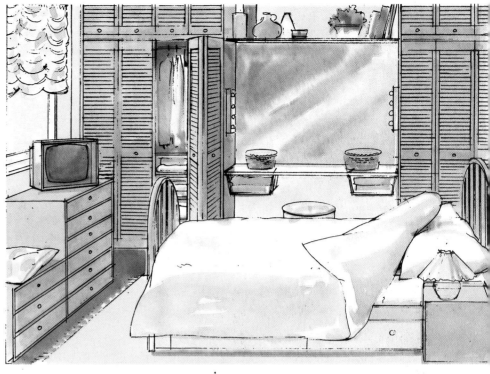

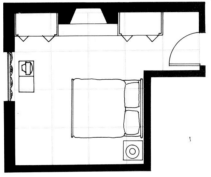

Scale: 1 square = 1 metre

◁ *Country simplicity*
Natural wood was chosen for the free-standing furniture in this attractive bedroom – a good choice to go with the pine fireplace. The full-length wardrobe has a concealed storage area in the base. There is a tall chest of drawers for clothing, with room for a mirror, lamp and pictures on top, and there is plenty of space to keep make-up in a two-drawer table.

△ *Fitted out*
In the alternative arrangement, fitted wardrobes with bi-fold, louvred doors are built in to the recesses on either side of the chimney breast. These fold-back panels slide on tracks and come as narrow as 30cm – useful if you are short of floor space. Louvred pine helps to provide texture and break up a large expanse of wood.

Wardrobes need to be 60cm deep – deeper than the recesses – so a slim dressing table fits neatly in between. It has wire trays on both sides for make-up, while film-star style bulbs on either side of the recess provide perfect light for making up.

Notice how the line of the picture rail continues across the front of the units. Above picture rail level, top cupboards with matching louvred doors provide space for rarely used items or out-of-season clothes.

BRIGHT IDEA

A small wall safe disguised as an electric plug socket is a cunning place to hide jewellery, documents or other valuables. Fitted into the skirting board – or anywhere else where a normal socket would look right – the heavy-gauge steel safe hides behind the false plug socket front and is locked and unlocked through one of the 'plug' pin holes. Install following the manufacturer's instructions.

CONFUSING THE BOUNDARIES

If your main bedroom is small, probably the last thing you want to do is to steal yet more floor space for large wardrobes. But you can have the best of both worlds – lots of storage and, at the same time, create the illusion of space by using clever colour schemes and mirrors.

Using colour As a rule of thumb, the paler your colour scheme, the more spacious the effect. Steering clear of using too many colours or large patterns helps too.

If you decide on built-in wardrobes, choose a light wood rather than a dark one, otherwise you will have a dark wall of doors dominating the rest of the room. And remember that louvred doors have a lighter feel about them than solid ones.

Another solution is to paint the doors so that the wardrobes melt in with the surrounding decoration. Or you could cover them with wallpaper to match the rest of the room, sealed with a protective coat of clear varnish.

Mirror effects Mirrors make space seem larger. A mirrored surface not only provides a looking glass for dressing but, if it is adjacent or opposite a window, increases the amount of light in the room.

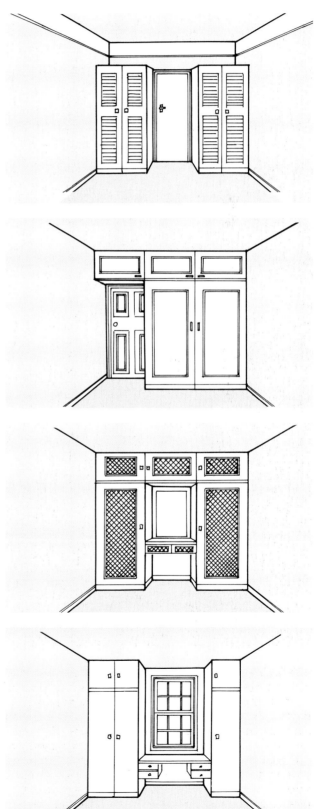

◁ **White space**

Mirrored wardrobes and an almost white scheme make this small room seem spacious and airy. As it is not overlooked, sheer festoon blinds are used to maximize all available light. Continuous surfaces – rather than lots of separate pieces of furniture – help to streamline things. Here, one top links three chests of drawers, creating a dressing table. One chest overlaps the window alcove and the top continues along the side of the bed, and incorporates a bookshelf.

▷ **Space-saving ideas** Top to bottom:
☐ Tall cupboards placed on either side of the door are neat and unobtrusive.
☐ In this room the door is to the side so a wide wardrobe with top cupboards and extra storage above the door is a good choice.
☐ An arrangement of cupboards and overhead storage to incorporate a dressing table and mirror.
☐ A window wall of cupboards and dressing table; mirroring the sides of the cupboards makes the window appear larger and gives more light.

△ Pull down

When space is really tight, open doors are a nuisance. These venetian blinds across one short wall are a neat solution. Behind them there is a flexible arrangement of hanging rails, shelves, drawers, and racks of wire vegetable baskets that can be wheeled out easily. Pleated paper or pinoleum roller blinds are cheaper alternatives to venetian blinds while, for a softer look, curtains hung from a ceiling track could be used.

BRIGHT IDEA

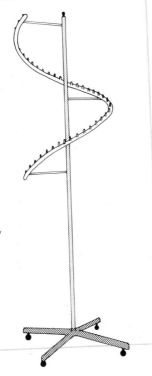

A spiral rail like those used in clothes shops is a good way to store shirts, dresses, jackets and trousers in a very limited space.

The spiral version will fit into a much smaller space than the more usual straight dress rail. It is 2m high but only 60cm in diameter and will take up to 60 garments of varying length.

This is not the sort of item you can buy from any high street outlet. Look in your Yellow Pages under the heading of Shopfitters.

△ Drawer space

You may have no space to fit a chest of drawers against a wall, perhaps because there is a radiator or door in the way, or you may simply need lots of drawer storage. A low chest positioned at the end of the bed like an ottoman gives you plenty of room for clothes and doubles as a seat or a convenient place for a TV.

BEDROOM LIGHTING

Bedroom lighting needs to be practical as well as able to produce an inviting atmosphere.

Bedroom lighting should be adaptable enough to combine good overall illumination with bright task lighting and softer, mood lighting to create a cosy atmosphere.

General principles At least one light should switch on from the door so that you don't have to stumble across a dark room. And it is much better if general lights can be controlled from the bed as well as the doorway.

Whether or not you are an avid reader-in-bed, you need good bedside lighting for getting into and out of bed. If you have to get up in the night it is more convenient, and less disturbing for anyone else in the room, to switch on a bedside lamp rather than the main light.

Dimmer switches are a valuable addition to bedroom lighting as they enable you to change the level of light to suit your mood.

Bedtime reading
The arc of light cast by a bedside lamp depends on the height of both the lamp base and the table on which it stands. Below, a short lamp on a high table provides just enough light for comfortable reading in bed. Above, if you have a lower table you'll need a taller lamp for easy bedtime reading.

CHOOSING THE FITTINGS

Most light fittings are perfectly suitable for bedrooms; your choice depends on your taste and needs.

A central pendant can give reasonable – but fairly inflexible – general illumination. One problem, however, is shadows; if you undress standing between the light and unlined curtains or a blind you may provide your neighbours with an interesting spectacle!

Wall lights strategically positioned round the room create warm pools of light. Two can be used as bedside lights, helping to give unity to your lighting scheme.

Downlighters Recessed downlighters provide good overall lighting, although you may have a problem with glare; the eye tends to be drawn towards the ceiling when lying in bed. You can overcome this by choosing downlighters with louvres or try the adjustable eyeball type. These can be angled towards the walls to highlight pictures or objects on shelves, or directed towards wardrobes or dressing tables. Wall-mounted spot-lights can also be used in this way.

▽ *Fold-away*
This swing-arm wall light is classic enough to work in both a period setting or a more tailored room. It is an excellent choice for the bedside as it can be folded against the wall or pulled round for reading.

△ *Classic lamp*
Wall lights are a particularly neat solution to the space problem in a small room and there are numerous styles from which to choose. The design of this lamp is based on an old-fashioned gas bracket fitting.

▽ *Flexible arrangement*
Downlighters unobtrusively complement the decor in a tailored bedroom. The ceiling lights and the two lights over the bedhead are each switched separately, and dimmers allow for changes of mood.

△ **Standard lamps**
If there is not enough space for a bedside table, a standard lamp provides a practical alternative. Its extra height gives a wide spread of light.

BRIGHT IDEA

Clamp-on lamp The simplest way of lighting the bedside is to use a clamp-on lamp attached to the bedhead. To prevent the clamp from damaging the bedhead, insert a piece of foam between the two.

LIGHTING THE BED

Table lamps to match the room's decoration are a popular choice. If you intend to use them as reading lamps, they need to be on fairly tall bases so as to shed light on your book.

Sometimes, however, there is not enough space for even the smallest bedside table or a lamp as well as all the necessary clutter. Wall-mounted fittings are one answer; pendants suspended over bedside tables are another space-saving idea.

△ *Double direction*
If you have space for large tables beside the bed you can choose imposing lamps with big shades. Little light is diffused through these opaque shades but, because of their height and the width of the bottom opening, they give excellent illumination over a wide area. They also cover the wall with light through the top aperture.

▷ *Versatile work light*
The no-nonsense lines of this adjustable task light suit this modern interior. Such a lamp is also extremely practical. Its jointing – based on that of the human arm – makes it easy to move into a variety of positions. It can be angled over the bed and adjusted up and down. The head can also be turned round to give indirect background illumination.

BEDROOM FURNITURE

Take your time choosing furniture and your bedroom can become something more than just a room to sleep in.

If the bedroom were used solely for sleeping, it would be the simplest of rooms to furnish, needing no more than the best bed money can buy. But it is also the place for storing clothes and personal effects, where you dress and make up, drink early morning tea, and read or watch television late at night. More than that, it often has to double up as a study/workroom, a children's playroom and, in small 'studio' flats, as the living room as well.

Furniture that performs so many roles must be flexible: in a bedroom/ study, for example, a desk with drawers and a wall-mounted mirror above would be more useful than a specialized dressing table. For those who eat breakfast, write letters, or watch TV in the bedroom, an additional table is needed. Good storage is always essential and you should never underestimate the space you will need for out-of-season clothes, blankets and linen, as well as books, records and other odds and ends. Space must also be found for those items – such as a radio, reading light, alarm clock, toiletries and so on – which are best kept on view.

If you are starting from scratch, you are free to choose from either built-in or freestanding ranges. Built-in furniture, which can be fitted into odd corners or angles, is often a good buy for small and oddly-shaped bedrooms. Larger or more regularly-shaped rooms can take advantage of the flexibility that a freestanding arrangement can offer. Combining the two options can give you the best of both worlds, particularly if you have existing pieces to incorporate.

Before buying, shop around for sizes and shapes to suit your bedroom, and colours and finishes to complement the look you want to achieve: stripped or varnished pine for a cosy cottage bedroom; rich polished mahogany in a large Victorian home; cool white melamine or pale blonde ash for simple masculine rooms; pastel drag-painted wood for a more romantic, feminine air.

Fitted elegance
Modern fitted wardrobes in plain white with a gold trim combine well with an old-fashioned brass bedstead.

BEDS AND SEATING

Beds are by nature conspicuous and cumbersome objects. There's no way really to prevent the bed dominating the room, especially when it is a double that needs space at either side for both occupants to get in and out.

The type you choose depends on the style and use of room – a simple divan for a modern interior; a brass or wood bedstead in a period home; bunk beds for children; a sofa bed for guests.

A practical and pretty headboard can be added very cheaply. A pair of piped foam cushions mounted on a pole or a padded fabric 'sleeve' to cover an old wooden headboard can be made to match the decor. Buying a headboard with a new bed makes it easier to match the style; the choice ranges from classic button-back upholstered headboards to cottage-style pine, natural or painted wicker, tubular steel, or sleek laminate.

Seating The minimum you need is a stool or chair for the dressing table and perhaps a small button-back 'lady's chair' on which to leave clothes over-night. A small sofa or armchair will turn a large bedroom into a haven for quiet moments away from the family.

△ **An imposing style**
Carved hardwood furniture suits this period bedroom, echoing the beamed ceiling. Two bedside table lamps allow one occupant of the bed to read while the other is sleeping, and an antique towel rail is both decorative and useful.

◁ **A choice of bedside tables**
A practical bedside table should have spacious drawers or shelves as well as generous surface space. A balustrade stops things slipping off and a pull-out surface forms a handy tray for early morning tea. A bedside table which is an integral part of the headboard makes for clean lines, while an extra-tall table makes reading in bed easier.

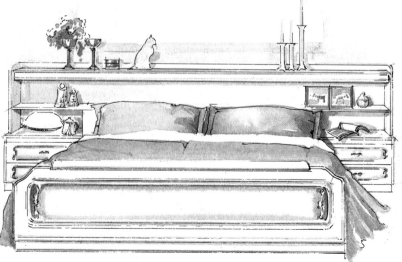

◁ A successful mixture
One advantage of freestanding bed-room furniture is that various styles and materials can be combined. Here a pine wardrobe and chest of drawers go well with a colourful modern sag bag, white bedstead and bedside table and a low, antique-looking table for pot plants.

▽ A bold design
A wardrobe fitted into an alcove makes excellent use of space, while a blanket box provides storage as well as seating. The vibrant colours in the bedding are picked up in the carpet and blind.

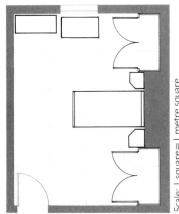

Scale: I square= I metre square

WARDROBES AND STORAGE

If you plump for built-in wardrobes, and have the space, you could dispense entirely with additional furniture, making the dressing table and bed an integral part of the design. A fitted bed surround can incorporate the headboard and tables, with high cupboards above for extra storage.

While freestanding wardrobes offer less storage space, they can be a better choice in an older home with fine original mouldings which would be obscured by built-in furniture. With the increased popularity of fitted furniture, there are plenty of second-hand bargains — junk shops and newspaper ads are great sources of well-made wardrobes in need of no more than a wash-down, polish or coat of paint. Look out for old doors, too, that a carpenter could build in as a cupboard door across an alcove.

A traditional storage item, such as an ottoman or blanket box, is a worthwhile addition for housing clothes and linen. Placed at the end of a bed, it can also double-up as an extra surface for a portable television or tea tray.

△ **Airy and light**
The clean, uncluttered design of this fitted furniture makes a relatively small bedroom seem spacious, yet manages to accommodate a surprising amount of storage space at the same time.

The line of the low drawers and cupboards is continued around the bed by a single shelf, with integral bedside lights. Although they are in fact separate pieces of furniture, the bed and split-level night table appear to be a single unit.

▷ **Bed alcove**
By using built-in furniture in this bedroom, it has been possible to create a whole wall of wardrobes, with a separate 'his' and 'hers' combination flanking the bed. High cupboards frame the bed and provide additional storage for out-of-season and rarely-used clothes.

DRESSING TABLES

When choosing a dressing table,
bear in mind the lighting and
storage arrangements as well as
the style of the table.

A dressing table can be practical – a place for making up, doing your hair and storing cosmetics and jewellery, as well as hairdryers, heated rollers and other similar equipment.

On the other hand, a dressing table can be more frivolous. As well as displaying scent bottles and elegant hair brushes, the table itself can add atmosphere and character to a bedroom.

So it's a good idea to start by asking yourself why you want a dressing table, and what sort of look you want to achieve. Then you can look around at the many types available in order to choose one which suits you, your lifestyle and your bedroom.

Setting the style The traditional kidney-shaped dressing table, often with a flounced fabric covering, is both elegant and practical. The curved shape allows a chair to be tucked neatly away; the fabric cover can usually be parted in the centre for access to drawers.

Many fitted bedroom ranges include a dressing table which can stand on its own or slot into place between other elements, giving the whole room a co-ordinated feel.

A freestanding chest of drawers, whether modern or antique, can easily double as a dressing table if a mirror is placed on top. The only real disadvantage is that, without a knee-hole, sitting down to use the mirror is less comfortable. Choose a chest of drawers which is high enough to use the mirror when standing.

Romantic glow
This long-skirted dressing table is covered in the same gingham fabric used for the soft furnishings.

A pair of tall table lamps shed ample light, the 'skirt' can be pulled aside to reach the drawers behind and the top is protected by glass. The result is a practical spot for making up which is in keeping with the delicate atmosphere of the bedroom.

LIGHTING

Lighting a dressing table and mirror is notoriously difficult. Daylight is best for making up and so many people place their dressing table near a window.

A pair of lamps, either standing on the dressing table or fixed to the wall at roughly eye level, will cast balanced artificial light. Avoid coloured lampshades which distort the light.

A single fluorescent strip above a dressing table casts shadows; it's better to opt for two strips, one on each side of the mirror. Choose 'colour corrected' fluorescent tubes. Hollywood-style lighting, with bulbs encircling the mirror, gives strong clear light.

The mirror should be close enough to use comfortably – a small extra mirror attached to an extendable arm is useful. According to the experts, eye make-up is best applied looking down into a hand mirror laid on a flat surface.

STORAGE

Plenty of drawers and shelves will prevent your dressing table from degenerating into a junk store. A cutlery divider will keep cosmetics neat and tidy. And if you plan to use any electrical gadgets – hairdryers, heated rollers and so on – place the dressing table near a power point so that flexes don't trail across the floor.

▽ *Practical co-ordination*
This dressing table – which is part of a range of modular bedroom furniture – provides masses of storage space to help keep the bedroom spick and span. It also benefits from ample natural light which can be finely adjusted by means of a venetian blind. A flexible table lamp provides additional light at night. The side wings of the three-panel looking glass can be adjusted for a good view.

◁ **Old and new**
Ranges of modular bedroom furniture allow you to choose a dressing table which best suits your needs. Here, the knee-hole dressing table in the room on the far left has been replaced by a taller chest of drawers.
   Tall candlestick lamps, an antique mirror and a pink colour scheme create a slightly less functional feel.

▽ **Side lights**
Strips of light bulbs such as these are available in kit form and are therefore relatively easy to install – either on both sides of a mirror, or along the top as well. It's best to fit at least two strips; a single strip would cast distorting shadows.

◁ **Hollywood style**
A series of naked light bulbs around a semi-circular mirror fixed to the wall produce excellent artificial light for making up. Light sources all round the face provide strong illumination without casting any shadows.
   Dark polished wood, shiny metal fittings and a series of small glass shelves make this dressing table both sophisticated and functional.

Improvisation Almost any table can serve as a dressing table, although one with a knee-hole and side drawers is best. If the table itself is old or worn, disguise it with a floor-length drape. Keep the fabric in place, and protect it from spills and stains, with a piece of thick glass with bevelled edges.

△ **A unique combination**
An elaborate Edwardian overmantel and the base of an old treadle sewing machine have been put to novel use as a dressing table. The entire construction has been painted lacquer red, black and yellow and teamed with cheerful patchwork-effect fabrics in the same colours.

▷ **Fresh from the country**
This pine side table serves well as a simple dressing table; it has been placed near a large window to gain maximum daylight. The free-standing cane mirror is hinged at the sides so that it can be tilted for a better view.

ATTIC BEDROOMS

As well as providing much needed additional space, a bedroom in the attic has its own special advantages.

An attic room tends to have a different feel from other bedrooms. It is usually the warmest place, as heat rises, and has a degree of privacy not possible in the rest of the house. It is rarely overlooked and often has an attractive bird's eye view of the surrounding area.

An attic bedroom must have a fixed staircase – a folding ladder leading to a hatch will not do. But the stairs can be narrow and twisting, or even spiral, check your local planning regulations.

DECORATION

Choose a scheme which makes the attic bedroom look more spacious. In general, small patterns work best and light colours are more suitable than dark – unless you want a dramatic effect.

Whether you treat the sloping areas as walls or ceiling depends largely on what proportion of the room is pitched. A large expanse of flat ceiling can be treated separately from slopes and wall but if there is little true ceiling, both areas are best handled as one. If there is a low area of flat wall below the slopes you could treat this as a dado and paint or paper it to accent the main pattern or colour.

If you want to carry the same wallpaper up one wall, across the ceiling and down the other side, choose a random or abstract pattern. If a design has a definite right way up on one side of the room it will turn disconcertingly upside down on the other and you may get a jarring effect where a flat end wall meets the ceiling. Instead, choose an allover design of flowerheads, a mini-print or a small geometric pattern.

Romantic roses
Here a floral wallpaper has been used for walls and slopes with a simpler, complementary design on the ceiling. The two areas have been clearly separated by adding a cornice in an accent colour. The window is pretty and high enough to be left uncurtained.

CONVERSION

If you need an extra bedroom, a loft or attic may be ideal for conversion. Some types of roof construction easily lend themselves to conversion, others make the job more difficult or even impossible.

You may need planning permission and, in any case, you are subject to building regulations which set down minimum standards as to headroom, size of windows, access and so on.

Windows The most easily installed windows are those which follow the roof profile. These can take the form of flush windows let into the roof slope, often with a central pivot for opening. Or fit windows in the vertical gable ends – casement, sash, pivot, round portholes or even triangles echoing the gable – to suit the exterior style of the house.

Dormers have the advantage of giving you extra headroom but involve a little more structural work. They also need careful handling in order not to spoil the overall look of the house. One small dormer, roofed and gabled to sympathize with the existing structure can be a very attractive feature; a long dormer incorporating windows and flat areas of wall needs more thought to avoid giving the house a top heavy appearance.

USING THE SPACE

Part of the attraction of an attic bedroom is its irregular shape – sloping ceilings, unusual windows and interesting nooks and crannies.

Often the usable area is long and rather narrow which offers several options. You may decide on two bedrooms, or one larger bedroom together with its own bathroom.

Another possibility is to have just one long bedroom incorporating a seating area or study.

You may find there are existing features which naturally split the room, perhaps a chimney stack or beams. Alternatively, you can use the windows to create a division; a window midway along one sloping wall could separate a seating area from a sleeping alcove.

Storage Because of their low, sloping ceilings, attics often have wasted space where there is not room to stand upright. But this space can make useful storage; cupboards built into the eaves have the advantage of being unobtrusive.

If you need taller hanging space than is possible with an eaves cupboard, you could build in cupboards along a window wall, with low cupboards under the windows and ceiling height wardrobes for the rest of the run.

◁ **Working space**
In this bedroom/study the sloping walls
and the ceiling and floor have been
close-boarded and painted gloss white
to make the most of the available light.

Generous built-in cupboards, which
accommodate the slope of the ceiling,
separate the sleeping and dressing area
from the desk and chair.

The bed fits neatly into the space
between the two runs of tall cupboards
under one window; its headboard
incorporates a wide shelf for a lamp,
books and so on. Under the far window
there is a cupboard to sill height for
papers and office clutter.

▷ **Teenager's den**
The same attic with one of the built-in
wardrobes removed has been
transformed into a bed/sitting room,
ideal for a teenager. A small desk with
an angled work lamp and chair under
one window provides a study, while
inexpensive modular seating under the
other window creates an area for
entertaining. Tubular steel shelving for
books and TV is a neat storage solution.

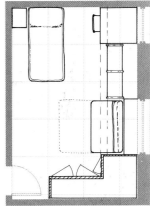

scale: I square = I metre

◁ **Under the eaves**
To overcome the height
problem of a floor-to-ceiling
slope, a cupboard is built into
the lower part of the wall.
The attic is painted to match
the sky – the walls, ceiling
and woodwork are bright
blue for bold impact. Crisp
white is used for the chair,
bed, table, cupboards and
wall lights.

The curtains are made of
white voile, cased top and
bottom and threaded on to
white-painted rods. The
bedlinen is hand decorated:
fabric paint was sponged on
to plain white sheets and
pillowcase to create clouds.

WINDOW DRESSING

One advantage of an attic bedroom is that it is rarely overlooked, so the window treatment can be purely decorative.

Dormers can be an attractive feature but, as they are often quite deeply recessed, some daylight is cut out of the room. Conventional curtains, even when drawn right back, still cover part of the window, cutting out even more light.

A roller blind is a practical choice but, used on its own, even a patterned blind looks quite severe and is best suited to tailored schemes. Frilly festoons, or roman blinds are softer looking. If there is space above to hang the blind, this will help make the window look taller.

Conventionally hung curtains and blinds are no good for sloping windows. Roller blinds on side runners are a neat solution, as are lengths of sheer fabric threaded on to curtain wire or rods, or curtains hung in the normal way at the top and held against the wall with a horizontal pole.

▷ *Tailored look*
Clear pastels and geometric designs create an unfussy setting for wooden furniture. A striped white roller blind reinforces the crisp, tailored theme and pale grey paper in the dormer recess makes the most of the available light.

◁ *Soft drapery*
As this attic room is not overlooked, the curtain is solely for decoration. A length of sheer fabric is hung across the window from a brass pole and then caught up at one side and allowed to spill liberally over the floor. Together with the leafy houseplant, this creates a pretty focal point without cutting out any daylight.

BRIGHT IDEA

Full length curtains Sloping windows can present difficulties when hanging curtains. Fix a curtain pole above the window and a second just below the slope. Hang the curtains from the top pole and tuck them behind the other one so that they follow the sloping lines of the wall.

△◁ Jagged edge

Hanging curtains on swivel rods on pivoting brackets is an excellent idea for a dormer window.

Here, salmon pink, green, grey and white striped fabric has been used. The curtains are taken right up to the ceiling and the space above the window is covered in the same fabric. Pink and green are alternated for the lining and the unusual saw tooth edging.

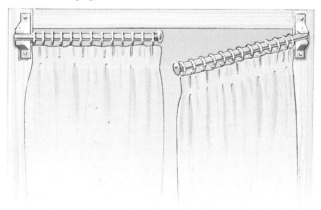

△ **Swivel rods** Curtains are slotted on to the rods or hung from runners. Each rod is swivelled across the window at night, opening back against the sides of the recessed window during the day. They can meet at the middle, as above, or cross over for a more luxurious effect. The curtains can be caught back with ties to follow the shape of the recess.

CORNERWISE

The steep slopes of a bedroom in the roof often create unusual corners which, at first glance, seem too awkward to be of any great use. Have another look and you'll find all sorts of ways to handle them.

Fitting in shelves is extremely easy and a display area does not need parallel, or even symmetrical, sides to look attractive. A sloping space too low for a chest of drawers, could house a blanket chest, toy box or even a child's desk and chair.

▷ Desk space
In this child's room, a sloping corner space has been turned neatly into a tiny study. A raised platform defines the area, the back is hung with shallow shelves, and a small wall-hung desk and stool take up the rest of the space.

▽ Boldly bordered
Painting the dado the same deep colour as the carpet and keeping the sloping wall above light gives a more spacious feel to a cramped space. A positive feature is made of the room's steep slope and angles by outlining each wall with a wallpaper border.

Mitring a border

1 Paste a length of border along one edge to within 25cm of corner. Extend unpasted section beyond corner and fold extending edge away from but following the angle of the next edge so you get a crease across the apex of the corner.

2 Cut along creased line, using a metal ruler and craft knife.

3 Fold and cut the next length in the same way, matching pattern on the fold.

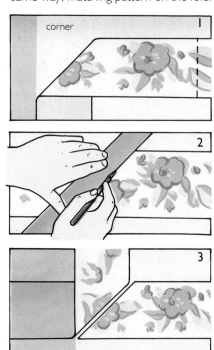

ROOM FOR A GUEST

With forethought, a spare bedroom can be warmly welcoming for guests and serve family needs at other times.

Having friends or relatives to stay can be a great pleasure for all, but careful thinking through is necessary in order to make the visit welcoming for your guests and worry-free for you. Most houses haven't space for a room specially set aside for visitors; often the spare room has to be put to use at other times, too. But with a little preliminary thought, these different roles can be successfully combined.

The atmosphere of a guest room is important. To provide a fitting welcome, the room should be fresh and inviting without being overwhelmingly forceful in style. Creating pleasantly comfortable surroundings needn't involve a heavy financial outlay. You don't have to buy expensive new furniture, though do avoid using the room as a dumping ground for ill-matched bits and pieces discarded from other areas of the house.

Your guests have chosen to spend time in your home, so don't feel you have to eradicate all traces of person-ality from the room. A dreary, hotel-like atmosphere, anonymously bland, may offend no-one but it won't actually give much pleasure, either.

It's the little touches which so often make guests feel especially welcome, rather than luxuries such as an en-suite bathroom. Pander just a bit to regular visitors. If children frequently stay you could collect together a surprise toybox or a drawer of modelling clay, crayons and puzzle books. For guests who rise earlier and retire later than the household, provide tea-making facilities and the loan of a TV or radio.

A big bowl of sweet-smelling flowers (especially if they are from your own garden) will make guests feel really very special.

A temporary haven
A fresh and inviting environment thoughtfully kept clear of the clutter that can so easily collect in a spare room. If you have space, twin beds provide the greatest flexibility of sleeping arrangement for guests.

AND SO TO BED

The bed can make or mar a visit for the guest, and it will almost certainly be one of your first considerations. Will you normally be having couples to stay? Do children often visit? Would you be better off with a double bed, or two singles? Single divans are generally more flexible as they adapt easily to different arrangements.

Experiment with the positioning of single beds, perhaps by placing them at right angles rather than side by side. Some single divans zip together for double comfort, and there are two-tier trundle beds; the lower one pulls out when needed.

Dual-purpose sleeping arrangements include sofa beds that sleep one or two people and chair beds that convert to sleep one. To keep floor space clear consider beds that fold up, or pull-down beds that store flat against a wall. Futons can fold up for seating, and roll out to form a bed. A regular shake will keep them loosely comfortable. Remember, though, elderly guests may have problems with a low bed.

Some sofa beds use the matching duvet as a daytime cover, but arrange convenient storage if bedding has to be removed during the day. A blanket box is ideal as it could hold extra blankets for chilly nights and also be used as a bedside table. Provide a light for bedtime reading, with a switch near the bed.

△ **Doubling up**
Single divans placed at right angles leave more floor space free than side-by-side positioning. With cushions and a cover, they adapt easily to a daytime seating arrangement.

▽ **Two into one**
Single beds that zip-link can be used as two singles or one double, whichever your guests prefer. It's a good idea to provide a radio or television, particularly if the stay is lengthy.

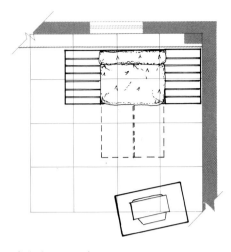

Scale: 1 square = 1 metre square

▽ ▷ **A welcoming home**
The inviting room shown below
cheerfully reflects the personality of the
household. A chest is a particularly
versatile piece of furniture for a
spare room, and little extras such as
the plants make it all a very cosy
temporary home.

As an alternative to the cane bed, a
futon (shown right) could flexibly meet
sleeping or seating needs. A light with
dimmer switch has been thoughtfully
positioned so that it can be used for
bedtime reading or general lighting.
And a television is bound to please.

DOUBLE PLEASURE

If you haven't the space to set aside a room specially for guests, consider furnishings that are flexible enough for double-up use. Beds for guests can provide daytime seating which will serve family needs at other times.

If the room has a dual role you may not want to fill available space with a wardrobe and chest of drawers. For guests' clothes you could partition or curtain off a wire storage system providing hanging space and trays for sweaters and so on. If you want to retain some storage for family use, keep it clearly defined in one area. For small rooms, a bentwood hatstand or a good supply of hangers for a series of coat hooks behind the door will be adequate for overnight visitors.

Choose versatile furniture for other purposes – a blanket box could be used as a bedside or occasional table, or convert a desk into a dressing table by adding a table-top mirror.

It's unlikely that many households will be able to offer guests the luxury of an en-suite bathroom. If they are to share family facilities, let them know the off-peak times so they can use the bathroom at leisure. A wash basin, screened from sight in the spare room, would ease pressure on the bathroom, and would doubtless be used at other times by the family. Keep guest towels warm and aired on a rail clipped to the radiator in the spare room.

Finally, before welcoming guests, put your spare room to the test by sleeping in it yourself for a night or two.

△ ▷ *Bedding down*
A sofa bed is particularly appropriate for a dual-purpose room as it converts quickly when guests come to stay and provides useful seating at other times. The mechanism of modern sofa beds is usually easier to operate than that of earlier models. If space is tight, look out for a sofa bed with storage for bedding built under the seating.

△ ▽ Ship-shape

Another versatile scheme that converts smoothly from night to daytime use. A ship-style bunk makes an attractive sleeping area and incorporates useful drawers for tidying away bedding during the day. This arrangement provides an unobtrusive sleeping area when guests stay the night; when visitors depart, it converts back for family use.

▽ Single style

Sleeping arrangements needn't dominate a room. Here furniture handsome enough for a study or second reception room can also meet the needs of an overnight guest.

◁ **Traveller's rest**
A colourful welcome awaits the guest who comes to stay in this home. Your visitors are less likely to feel that they are living out of a suitcase if a space for bags and cases is provided. Here a high bedstead means they can be tucked neatly away under the bed.

▽ **Basin boon**
A wash basin in a spare room can be a boon for guests and ease the bathroom rush hour for the rest of the household. A screen or partition will keep wash facilities separate for visitors, and enable the room to be used for general family purposes.

A READY WELCOME
Often small things rather than luxuries will ensure a happy stay for your guests. Apart from the essentials – a comfortable bed with spare blankets, bedside light, clothes storage – a thoughtful hostess will have ready some of the following hospitality measures:

☐ facilities for making drinks – a small travel kettle or element and teabags; coffee, sugar, hot chocolate and creamer sachets; fresh water and milk
☐ mineral water and glasses
☐ a soluble analgesic
☐ a small sewing kit and scissors
☐ tissues
☐ a clock
☐ guest towel and soap, plastic shower cap, sachets of shampoo and foam bath plus toothbrush and toothpaste for emergency use
☐ a tin of biscuits
☐ a few general interest magazines and paperback books; short stories, cartoons, crossword puzzles
☐ folder with writing paper, envelopes, pen
☐ hot water bottle/electric blanket
☐ loan of a radio or TV

HIGHLIGHTING THE BED

The bed is the most dominant item in the bedroom so dress it up to become an attractive focal point.

The bedroom is the one room in the house where you can introduce a touch of real drama. The spotlight is on the bed, so turn it into the focal point of the room. There are many styles of bed treatment from which to choose, ranging from the luxury of a four-poster, draped with flowing curtains and maybe covered with matching bedlinen, to a more modern built-in arrangement.

FULLY FITTED

The built-in wardrobes and storage units which are so popular in bedrooms can be taken a step further. Shelves built up around and above the bedhead make a streamlined focal point and a convenient place for books and lamps – a practical and smart approach.

Another effective and simple way to give the bed importance is with careful use of colour and pattern. The top cover on the bed can bring a big splash of colour to your room. A bed covered in a strong coloured glazed cotton looks good against walls and a deep pile fitted carpet in a much paler contrasting colour.

WAYS WITH FABRIC

If you have set your heart on a more traditional look, you could choose a four-poster, draping it with masses of patterned fabric and picking out one colour from it for the walls, paintwork and window curtains. Or use just one colour for bed drapes, walls and curtains. If you want a light and airy effect, drape the bed with masses of sheer fabric or lace.

In a very small bedroom, an interesting idea is to treat bed and room as one, tenting the ceiling with fabric and covering the walls with paper in the same design.

Symmetrical arrangement
This dramatic bed treatment relies for its effect on strongly-coloured bedlinen and co-ordinating curtains in a geometric pattern. The bed is cleverly set between the two windows, framed by their curtains.

The walls, woodwork and flooring are all white, while the bedhead and table at the bottom of the bed in glossy black lacquer provide a sharp contrast. An abstract poster over the bed picks up the colours in the textiles and yellow venetian blinds echo the horizontal bands of colour on the duvet cover.

BUILT-IN

A bed built into, or surrounded by, a line of fitted cupboards or low-level storage units can look very effective. It is also extremely practical as bookcases and tables can be incorporated into the scheme and provide surfaces for telephones, books and treasured items.

Slotting the bed into a run of wardrobes also gives scope for lighting, and the space over the bed can be filled with a picture or mirror.

Alternatively, a storage system incorporating a bedhead as part of a run of low units makes a neat setting for the bed. Raising the bed on a platform has the double advantage of giving it more importance and, if drawers are fitted beneath, of providing storage space.

△ *Herringbone effect*

Sisal floor covering is used for the bed platform and drawers underneath and is continued partway up the walls, giving an interesting texture to this double bedroom.

Strips of sisal are stitched together and glued to the wall and platform surfaces. Notice how the edges have been covered with a shelf that runs around the bedhead, with a lower second shelf following the same lines to make a useful bedside table.

The illustration, right, shows the other end of the room. A built-in cupboard beside the doorway has a space-saving sliding front which incorporates a simple but useful dressing table.

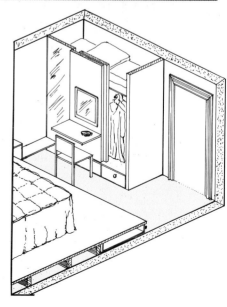

◁ *Usefully framed*
In this room the bed fits neatly into a built-in framework which also provides useful cupboards and surfaces on which to keep books and ornaments. The warm pink bedspread introduces a strong colour and, with the blue painting, focuses attention firmly on the bed.

▽ *Neat and elegant*
Here the bedhead is part of a low-level storage unit which provides a practical background for a double bed.
   The stark white quilt and bedlinen stand out against the pale wood and the greeny-grey carpet. At night, the bed is lit by downlighters, while in the daytime, the eye is drawn to the unusual sloping window above the bed.

IN ROMANTIC MOOD

When draping and swagging a bed it is essential to be lavish with fabric. Although it looks and sounds expensive, in fact quantity is far more important than quality.

Inexpensive fabrics which drape well – muslin, scrim, calico, poly-cotton sheeting, curtain lining or even ordinary dress fabric – can create a fabulous effect.

◁ Four-poster effect

You can easily create a four-poster effect without having a four-poster bed, as in this room where a frame reaching up to the ceiling is attached to the bed. It is draped with long curtains and more fabric is hung behind the bed and tented over it. The whole room – walls, paintwork, curtains and bed frame covering – is in the same pale cream which makes a fine setting for the patchwork quilt and tablecloth.

▷ Pretty accent

A semi-circular corona or half-tester is an attractive alternative to a four-poster and is one of the prettiest ways to accent the bed. Here the decorative treatment of the bed is reinforced by a matching valance over the window.

MAKING A FOUR-POSTER BED

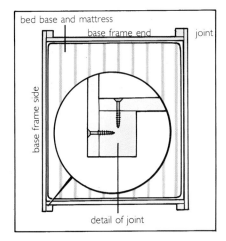

bed base and mattress
base frame end
joint
base frame side
detail of joint

△ Make a frame for the base of the bed

To make the base frame ends, measure the width of the bed and add 20mm to measurement to allow for some clearance between frame and bed. Cut two pieces of chipboard to this measurement, and to a width that will reach halfway up the bed base.

To make the base frame sides, measure the length of the bed and add 120mm to allow for the thickness of the corner posts and for clearance. Cut the chipboard to length and to the same width as the frame ends.

Cut four 230cm lengths of 50mm sq

softwood for the posts. Hold the posts upright. Screw the frame ends to the inner faces of the bottom of the posts as shown in the inset detail, then get a helper to hold them in position against the bed while you screw the frame sides securely to the outer faces of the posts to complete the frame.

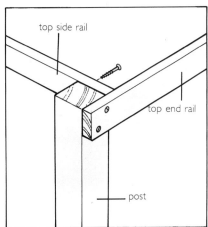

top side rail
top end rail
post

△ Make the top frame

Take four pieces of 50 × 25mm softwood. Cut two the same length as the base sides, and two the same length as the base ends. Attach them to the top of the corner posts.

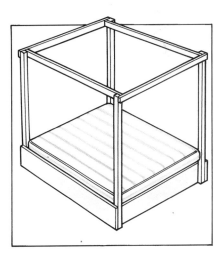

△ The finished frame

Once the frame has been built you are ready to decorate your four-poster bed.

Cover the base frame with fabric, attached by heavy-duty staples or tacks.

The upright posts can be painted, or you could attach a length of matching fabric to the top of each post, twisting it round like on a maypole.

Finally, tack swags of fabric to the top frame crossbars – the more fabric you use, the more luxurious the effect – and to complete the look, cover the top with a canopy.

△ Corner style
This bed is set out from the corner of the attic room at an angle. A patchwork quilt laid diagonally across the bed with edges spread out over the floor accentuates the look.

BRIGHT IDEA

Half-tester effect Swivelling dormer brackets can be used to make a simple half-tester. The tracks come with runners for curtain hooks but these can be removed if, as with sheers or lace, you want to slide the track through casing.

△ Colourful contrast
A bed set against plain coloured walls and neutral carpet is given importance with a bold bedspread and matching valance. Notice the attractive and unusual bedhead.

THREE STAGES TO A PERFECT BEDROOM

Let the bedroom of your dreams evolve gradually.

Considering the importance of a good night's rest to our general well-being, it's surprising that the bedroom is so often neglected. Yet it's a rare individual who hasn't some notion of an ideal bedroom – whether crisp restraint or a cocoon of romantic bedhangings – but how to work towards that end?

What can't be achieved all at once is often possible in well-considered stages – and there's no reason why you shouldn't have a comfortable bedroom at each stage. In a new home other things may take precedence, but draw up long-term plans so the room doesn't lose direction along the way. Shed things in an established bedroom that don't add up to a pleasing whole.

There are some basics common to every fine scheme. A good bedroom, and a good night's sleep, begins with a comfortable bed. In an existing bedroom, review your bed critically: is it due for retirement? If you need to buy a bed, buy a good one and make it a priority at an early stage.

Sweet dreams
A bedroom can be a perfect retreat from the rest of the world, but it's rare that a scheme that exudes luxury can be achieved all at once. Meticulous planning has gone into details of this room. A clever idea is the concealed lighting – which must be installed before soft furnishings are made up – to emphasize the corona and bed drapes, while a fine quilt and swags and tails combine to make a very special room.

PLANNED OPERATION

Stage 1 If your budget won't stretch to a top quality bed, sink your funds into a really good mattress and sleep on that, on the floor, for the time being. Improvise on a top cover: candlewick or a wool travelling rug, perhaps. Find a temporary way of dealing with storage: perhaps a screened clothes rail or curtained alcove, with hanging sweater and shoe holders to keep things tidy.

Buy a bedroom-quality carpet or a generous rug and sand and varnish the floorboards. A venetian blind softened by sheer side hangings is simple but effective for windows. Choose temporary lighting at this early stage – free-standing lights, and table lamps at the right height for bedtime reading. Freshen walls with a neutral colour until you decide what to do next.

Stage 2 Add a bed base for your good mattress if necessary. Storage needs should be obvious by now, so settle on a permanent plan – good fitted or freestanding wardrobes and drawers. Once the lighting is chased in – perhaps wall-mounted over the bed – repaint or paper walls in your favourite scheme. For low-cost softness drape windows with cheesecloth or muslin.

Stage 3 This is the point to surround yourself with whatever you feel makes life more comfortable. If you like, spend money on good soft furnishings – dress the bed with generous swathes of fabric. Give windows a top dressing of swags and tails.

If you prefer understated elegance, search out real quality in the details. Concentrate on one feature of the room: an antique iron bedstead or a distinctive old chest, perhaps. Replace plain venetian blinds with equally plain but rather more stylish roman blinds.

Find neat housing – possibly fitted cabinets – for a plethora of bedside electrics: lighting, a clock-radio, tea-maker, telephone. A TV on a trolley or swing-out shelf is unobtrusive when you don't want to view.

Country stages

A room that's grown in character is at first kept manageably simple (above). A good bed and carpeting are first-stage basics, with off-white painted walls for a low-cost, neutral background. A tied-back curtain uses fabric sparingly, with the same soft apricot on a candlewick spread – a colour that works well and is used again in later stages. A blanket box for stowing clutter has a temporary home under the window.

Stage 2 (below) introduces more furniture to evoke a country spirit: a sturdy washstand and the old chest of drawers – a junk shop find – that holds promise in spite of a covering of thick paint. The print that livened up a dull corner is replaced by a needlework sampler which exactly suits the mood.

At Stage 3 (left) the chest – now stripped and polished – lives up to its potential, with stencilling, brass handles and a mirror to complete the transformation. Finishing touches include soft furnishings. A rug softens the floor, and – a nice personal touch – a handpainted screen fronts the fireplace. The sampler is such a favourite that it takes a prime wall site.

△ ◁ Minimal flair

With the basics in place Stage 1 (above) is elegantly spare rather than sparse. The best mattress money will buy, handsome plain blinds and a carpet that's soft underfoot are the main first-stage expenses.

Stage 2 (left) has similar flair but with some extra comforts. Now the mattress has a bed base and headboard. Modern angled lights, ideal for bedtime reading, sit on units which run the length of the wall, encasing the radiator. An extra treat is the television which can be wheeled out to view from the bed or the comfortable new armchair.

With temporary curtained-off storage giving way to built-in wardrobes and the possibility of roman blinds at the window, in Stage 3 the room will be complete. Planned this way, there has been no compromise at any stage over looks or comfort.

Tranquil transition

After laying down the essentials – a good bed and soft flooring – in the first stage, a bedroom that's used in the daytime has been turned into a pleasant retreat with an armchair and fine old desk (above). The room is on the dark side so white bedcovers add a crisp freshness.

To relieve the subtle browns, another colour is introduced in the final stage (below): the rich green of the rug and corona makes the bed a distinctive centrepiece. A cheval mirror reflects light in a dull corner, brass swing-arm lights add extra style and pictures have been rehung to create focal points about the room.

BRIGHT IDEA

Well handled If you don't like the handles on a chest of drawers or cupboard, you can transform furniture quite easily by adding a set of new handles. Choose from a wide selection of plain or decorated ceramic, wood and brass styles to suit a modern or traditional setting.

△ **Mediterranean mood**
If you know you'll take a
while to build up from the
basics, go all out for
wholehearted simplicity. The
clearest of green paint with
pink-washed walls work
together like a dream here.
Comforts – a rug on the
floor, more permanent
lighting – can come later.
Unless, of course, you've
been won over by the bare
essentials!

▷ **Dual-purpose**
A bedroom that's used for
several purposes has smart
modular furniture that fits
awkward spaces and can
expand with possessions.
A judiciously placed blind
screens different functions.
Finishing details like the
roman blinds at the window
can be added as time goes
by. Harmony of colour has
evolved through the stages
to a particularly effective final
result.

NURSERIES: NEWBORN TO TWO

Babies and toddlers thrive in a warm, safe and attractive room of their own.

It isn't essential for a very new baby to have its own room, but after the first few weeks most people prefer to give him or her a separate nursery. This is best positioned close to the parents' room and away from the noise of the main living areas. A baby alarm in the kitchen or living room is a great help if you want to make sure the baby is sleeping without having to race up and down stairs.

People are inclined to think that a baby needs only a very small room, but your baby will not stay tiny for very long. The nursery needs to be adaptable to changing needs, and furniture and storage should be flexible. Miniature furniture may seem irresistible at first but is soon outgrown. A cot that can be converted into a bed, or a wardrobe with adjustable hanging rails for different sized garments is much more useful.

Decoration Plain colours or small print patterns for walls won't lose their appeal as quickly as a special nursery pattern that will be branded childish in a few years. Cushioned vinyl or cork flooring is warm to the touch, quiet to tiptoe across and easy to clean, and babies seem to prefer to crawl on a shiny surface.

Visual stimulus Babies are fascinated by colourful things and objects that move. You could make a mobile to hang over the cot, or hang pictures in view of it – change them regularly to make the display more interesting (see overleaf).

Playroom

This comfortable nursery has space for an armchair and has plenty of storage fitted into a wide alcove. There is room for a highchair and playpen and there is also lots of crawling space. The low cupboard can be turned into a toy store later.

ESSENTIALS

A crib, moses basket or removable carry-cot is cosier than a full-sized cot for a tiny baby. A moses basket or carry-cot is easy to carry and can be placed inside the big cot for convenience. This will also help to get the baby used to its future surroundings.

When buying a cot, choose a reliable make from a shop with a good reputation. Check its stability and make sure the dropside mechanism is safe and can't be worked by a toddler. A cot with an adjustable mattress position is a good idea. When the baby is very small, the cradle can be placed on the mattress at high level, saving parents' backache. Later on, the mattress can be lowered to prevent an active toddler from climbing out over the sides.

Once out of bed, small babies like to be propped up to see the world. A bouncing cradle or moulded plastic recliner with padded interior does this job well.

△ *Versatile room*

A well-planned nursery needs plenty of storage space. Here there is a small wardrobe with matching dresser – the top doubles as a changing table. A tall bookcase is used to display eye-catching toys, and later can be fitted with doors and used as clothes storage space.

▷ *Cot bumper*

Patterned padded bumpers securely tied to the cot protect a baby's head from the bars and draughts.

Parents spend a lot of time in a baby's room so, if there's space, add a comfortable old armchair.

Changing You need a surface at waist height for nappy changing, with storage to hand for all the essentials such as pins, powder and creams. There are purpose-made units available or use a changing mat on a table or chest, with a box or plastic cutlery tray close by for all the bits and pieces.

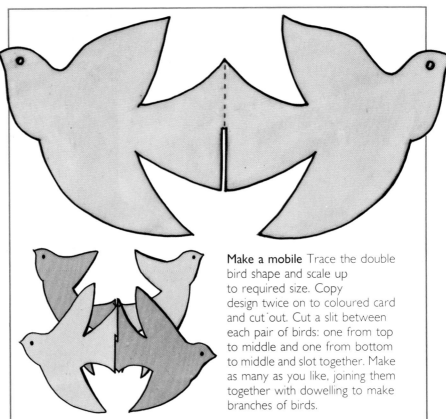

Make a mobile Trace the double bird shape and scale up to required size. Copy design twice on to coloured card and cut out. Cut a slit between each pair of birds: one from top to middle and one from bottom to middle and slot together. Make as many as you like, joining them together with dowelling to make branches of birds.

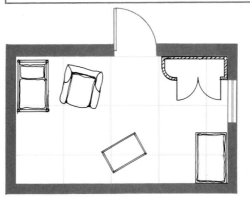

scale: 1 square = 1 metre

▽ *Adaptable furniture*
An old built-in wardrobe has been refitted with extra drawers and hanging rails to suit nursery needs. The top of the wooden chest-of-drawers is a good spot for the changing mat and the drawers beneath provide more storage. Both pieces can be painted the same colour for co-ordination.

STORAGE

For such small people, babies have a vast quantity of possessions. You need well-planned storage to stop the nursery, and indeed the whole house, becoming cluttered.

Most baby things are folded flat rather than hung, so in the early days a cupboard with drawers is more useful than a wardrobe.

Fitting out an alcove with shelves is less expensive than buying a new chest-of-drawers and more versatile: you can choose the depth and spacing to suit changing needs. Or you could transform a drab second-hand chest-of-drawers with a new coat of paint.

If you decide on a wardrobe or already have a built-in cupboard, it is probably more useful at this stage to remove the rail and fit the interior with shelves. You can adapt it later to suit the needs of a growing child, removing the lower shelves to take a toddler's toy box, clothes rail and so on.

A blanket box is another option and makes a good toy store and seat as the child grows older.

HEATING AND LIGHTING

Babies need to be kept warm; a room heat of 18-21°C is recommended. These days many houses have central heating, but if not, an approved electric convector heater is a suitable alternative.

A dimmer switch is very useful for a soft glow of light during night-time feeds and for checking on the baby. Out-of-reach wall or ceiling mounted lights are a better choice than plug-in table lamps with trailing flexes.

Getting a baby or toddler to go to sleep on light summer evenings can be a problem: lining curtains in an opaque, dark-coloured fabric, interlining them with a thick material, or supplementing the curtains with a light-obscuring blind are all good solutions.

△ **Room with a view**
There is plenty for a baby to look at in this nursery: a variety of objects on the shelves and a mobile in view of the cradle. A large, securely fixed mirror creates changing interest by reflecting the room.

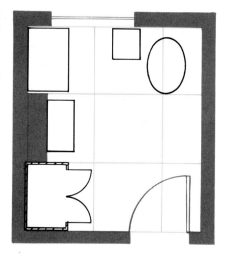

scale: 1 square = 1 metre

SAFETY

☐ Don't use pillows for babies – they might smother
☐ Don't put bars on windows – in case of fire
☐ Use safety glass in low windows or cover with safety film
☐ Use window locks to stop children falling out
☐ Never put cot or bed by a radiator
☐ Use proper guards for all fires (including electric and radiators)
☐ Never leave a baby (lying or in a seat) on a table or worktop
☐ Put furniture in front of socket outlets or, better still, use safety covers
☐ Don't have trailing electric flexes
☐ Fix a gate to the top and bottom of the stairs

BRIGHT IDEA

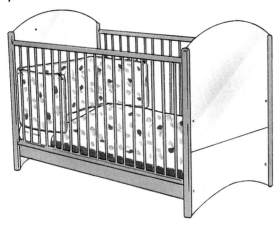

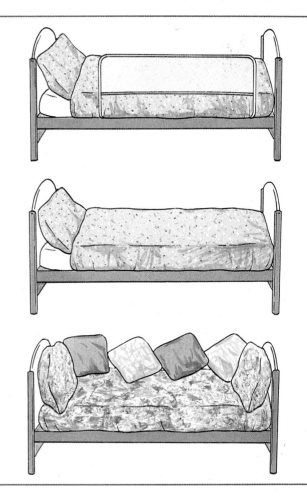

A convertible cot which has more than one mattress height is a good choice. This one is larger than average and converts into a bed which fits the child for several years.
☐ After the very early days the mattress is lowered, leaving the sides attached to stop an adventurous baby climbing out.
☐ For the first few months in a bed a soft mesh bedguard stops a toddler falling on to the floor.
☐ Eventually, with piled-up cushions, you can make it into a child-sized sofa. If you have more than one child, you probably won't want to convert the cot until the youngest is ready to sleep in a bed.

△ *Painted scene*
Small children like to look at interesting things. Here a fake open window painted on a blank white wall gives a view of a tropical sky and exotic birds.

◁ *Cut outs*
This decorative border just above the skirting is at the right height for a child to enjoy. Cutting out some motifs and grouping them on the wall gives an individual touch.

TODDLERS' ROOMS AND PLAY AREAS

Two- to five-year-olds need bedrooms
that are stimulating for play
as well as peaceful for sleeping.

A good time to reassess the sleeping arrangements of toddlers is when they are ready to move from cot to first bed, at around the age of two, especially if the original nursery is too small to accommodate a full-sized bed. While proximity to the main bedroom is a priority with a new baby, parents of an early rising toddler may prefer to put some distance between them for the sake of a few more minutes' peace in the mornings. Depending on the layout, the bedroom should ideally be situated away from the noise of the living room.

If you are planning a toddler's room from scratch, your main concerns should be safety, practicality and visual appeal – in that order.

Safety first Fearless toddlers can easily hurt themselves, turning innocent everyday items into potential hazards.

The same care you exercise when buying safe toys, non-toxic paints and crayons and so on, should be taken when choosing the furniture and furnishings for their bedrooms. Choose fitted or heavyweight furniture which cannot be pulled over and has no sharp edges; lead-free paint for re-vamping an old chest, bed or chair; child-proof locks for cupboards the contents of which you prefer left intact; safety covers for electric sockets; non-slip mats and floor-coverings; safety gates for adjacent stairways; and safety catches for windows so they don't open too far.

Make sure that toddlers' playthings are well within reach, or they may turn into mountaineers as they try to overcome the challenge of high shelves and cupboards. If you want to protect books and other precious or breakable items, try to store them in another room; if they have to go on high shelves in the room itself, provide a stable step or stool for an older child to reach them in safety.

A magical bedroom
Apart from its obvious charm, this enchanting hand-painted mural provides stimulation for a child's imagination and a starting point for stories and games. A similar, if less original, effect can be created with stencils.

DOS AND DON'TS

The guidelines below will help your toddler's room resist rough treatment.

Wallcoverings A toddler's room is no place for expensive finishes which can be heart-breakingly ruined at the stroke of a felt-tip pen. Washable vinyl paint is much more likely to keep its good looks and does not date in the same way as childrens' patterned wallpapers. Pictures, pinboards or murals can all introduce an element of pattern.

Floorcoverings Fitted carpets or carpet tiles are best for warmth and comfort, though not perhaps the most durable floorcovering for a toddler. An inexpensive carpet (a 'room-sized remnant', perhaps) with a high proportion of synthetic fibres, should wear well and some are treated to resist spills. Cork or vinyl tiles or sheet vinyl are more practical and can be warmed up with washable rugs, but avoid high-gloss

finishes and use a non-slip backing for the rugs.

Furniture 'Building-in' is a wise investment, as it is both secure and space-saving. One floor-to-ceiling cupboard should provide all the hanging space needed for small clothes; a series of shelves below for shoes and toys can be removed as the clothes become longer.

If the budget won't stretch to fitted furniture, choose sturdy freestanding pieces with a combination of hanging and drawer space. Nursery furniture is soon outgrown; re-vamped old furniture is practical and cheap.

Buy a standard-sized bed with a sprung mattress and safety guard rather than an uneconomical 'child bed'. And if you want a second bed for occasional visitors, trundle beds (where the extra bed is stored below the main bed) or perhaps a futon rolled up to become a sofa are preferable to bunk beds.

△ *A shared playroom/bedroom*
This room is decorated in primary colours – bright pictures and paper kites liven up the sunny yellow walls, and a rug protects the carpet.

Bunk beds save space where two children share a room, but it's best to allocate the top bunk to the older child. Low drawers and a miniature table and chairs complete the combined bedroom/playroom effect.

Storage A tidy toddler is a rare being indeed – but providing ample, accessible storage helps maintain some order. Open cubes and shelves, and plastic or wicker baskets are a good combination.

Lighting which is permanently fixed to the ceiling or wall is safest. Table or night lights should be used only if the flex is concealed or permanently attached to the wall and the socket is as child-proof as you can make it.

△ Circus stripes

In this shared bedroom, roomy cupboards below the bunk beds keep toys tidy, leaving the floor free for games.

•The decor is simple but effective – the panelling recreates the stripes of a circus tent and the furniture is painted a darker shade of blue. The varnished floor is tough and easy to clean.

▷ An alternative to bunk beds

Trundle beds are a practical space-saver where two children share a room; all that is needed is space for the extra bed to be rolled out. The window pane is covered with a clear plastic film which holds broken glass in place should an accident occur.

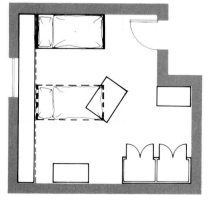

Scale: I square = I metre square

△ A room to grow up in

Children's tastes change as they grow up, and making drastic alterations to a toddler's bedroom to fit in with these changes can prove expensive!

This bedroom is eminently practical. The basic decoration is simple and will suit older children as well as toddlers, while the bright colours give it a cheery feel. Similarly, the furniture is adaptable – the large wicker chair is comfortable for a teenager or adult although the cushions make it cosy for a small child, and the chest under the windows can be turned into a dressing table. The low plastic table provides a spot for painting, jigsaws or tea parties.

▷ Woodland animals

Bedlinen designed specially for children makes a toddler's bedroom special and is not very expensive. There is a huge variety of designs and colours to choose from, often incorporating famous story book or television characters – it's a good idea to let toddlers choose their own. That way, they might be more willing to go to bed on time!

A PLACE TO PLAY

As toddlers begin to make friends, they are usually quite happy to spend more time playing with them in their own rooms. Making the room a pleasant and stimulating place to be will encourage this newly-discovered independence.

Growing toddlers may want to contribute their own decorative ideas, insisting on the presence of favourite book or TV characters. But since their tastes are bound to change, these are best kept to the cheapest elements (such as pictures and lampshades) with a fairly plain, though bright, background.

To be congenial, toddlers' bedrooms need to cater for the many activities likely to be crammed into a day. Allocating separate areas for different pastimes encourages children to move naturally from one to another. While messy activities are best confined to the kitchen, children like to display their creations on a pinboard or cork-covered wall. (Sticky tab fixings are safer than drawing pins.)

▷ **A practical arrangement**
Below the dado rail, Anaglypta wallpaper, painted with water-resistant paint, protects the walls of this tiny room. An attractive washable rug covers the hard-wearing carpet.

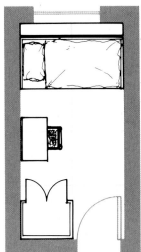

Scale: 1 square = 1 metre square

◁ **Space at a premium**
Often, the only way that toddlers or small children can be given their own room is by dividing a large room into two tiny ones. Here, a desk under the window provides a bright spot for painting or colouring and the bed ranged along one wall is matched by storage cupboards along the other.

▷ Keeping tidy

An adjustable storage system such as this is bright, attractive and likely to encourage toddlers to keep their possessions reasonably tidy. It is also sturdy enough to have a chance of retaining its good looks.

Stacking crates or vegetable racks, or wire trays in a metal frame are other cheap and cheerful alternatives to practical, see-at-a-glance storage for toys, games and books.

▽ Improvised storage

A wipe-clean melamine worktop (intended for kitchen use) has been installed in this toddler's room to provide an activity centre for painting, drawing and modelling.

A sturdy storage box mounted on castors is easy to roll out from under the worktop. Washable borders liven up both the worktop and the box.

BRIGHT IDEA

A safe stool is a boon wherever toddlers' legs simply aren't long enough. A stable but light plastic stool enables toddlers to step up into the bath or wash their teeth at the basin by themselves. It also has many uses elsewhere in the home – to sit on when drawing or painting at a low desk, as a stool for watching television, or to encourage toddlers to put away toys that belong in a high drawer.

CHILDREN'S ROOMS: FIVE TO TWELVE

This age group needs a well-designed space in which to grow and pursue a variety of activities.

Like everyone else, there are times when children need to get away from the rest of the family; to escape to a place which they can truly call their own.

In the average-sized home, two children sharing will often have to make do with a smallish room, while a third child may well have a room no bigger than an old-fashioned box room. And usually a child's room has to double up as a playroom.

This means available space must be utilized to its fullest extent. There will need to be places for hanging clothes, keeping toys, games, books and other paraphernalia, as well as for a bed. Ideally, there should be a work surface or table and a chair.

Furniture for children should be service-able but attractive and of a size to fit a child's needs for some years. It's no use spending money on tiny furniture for a five-year-old which will be quite in-appropriate by the time the child is eight or nine.

A full-height fitted cupboard is a good choice as the interior can be adjusted to suit changing needs. In the early days a double tier of hanging rails on one side means that the bottom rail is within a young child's reach. The other side can have storage boxes or baskets at floor level for toys, with shelves above for clothes, bedlinen and so on. Later on, remove the lower rail and the child can take over some of the shelves.

Small beds specifically designed for little children are rather a waste of money — a full-sized one is a far better investment. Bunk beds are very popular. They allow more play area in a shared room and are handy for an occasional guest in a single one.

Safety first Never put a child under five in a top bunk. At any age an adequate guard is necessary, and the ladder must be secure.

Large expanses of glass and active children do not go together. Try not to put a child in a room with windows below waist height; if this is unavoidable then use safety glass or hardboard for the low-level panes and add a single bar across at, or above, waist level. Don't position furniture so that adventurous children can climb up and fall out of windows.

Install safety guards over radiators and never use a free-standing heater in a child's room. Obviously, any fire should be well guarded. Trailing electric flexes are dangerous as they act like tripwires and wall sockets should be pro-tected with safety covers or positioned where a small child can't get at them.

Light and bright

A single room with a light and airy colour scheme in clear pastels. The large wardrobe gives plenty of storage and there is a roomy desk with drawers for papers, pens and pencils.

△ Room to dance

A large wardrobe with mirrored sliding doors takes clothes and clutter for this ballet enthusiast. Plastic hooks screwed to the wall on either side support a removable practice barre.

The colour scheme is a sunny yellow and white, accented with a strong blue.

An unusual feature is the bed canopy. A casing at one end of a length of fabric takes a pole which is tied to screw eyes fixed to the wall above the bedhead. Screw eyes fixed to joists in the ceiling above the four corners of the bed support poles hung from them with strong cord. The fabric is then draped over the poles and tucked into the bed end.

PAINT AND PAPER

Decorating a child's room is an enjoyable exercise and one where you can be bolder than in other parts of the house.

It may sound obvious, but do consult your child on his or her own decorative ideas. It's very easy to get carried away and to forget that it is not you who will be using the room. If the child has a particular hobby or interest you can use this as a theme. Don't overdo it – he or she might soon grow out of that particular craze.

Another pitfall is to make the scheme too finished and co-ordinated, leaving no scope for the child's own personality.

Decorative ideas Whatever sort of decoration you choose, go for wipeable surfaces for peace of mind all round. There are any number of well-designed wallcoverings and borders which are specifically for children, and many adult ones are also acceptable.

An area of black or white board with chalks or felt pens allows free expression which is easily wiped away, and a pinboard will hold drawings or posters.

▽ Art gallery

The same basic layout has been given a new slant based on a strong geometric fabric which covers the headboard, divan base, and disguises an old armchair. Colours from the fabric are used on one wall, desk and chair and bedlinen. Another wall is covered in cork tiles to picture rail height and becomes an ever-changing art gallery.

BRIGHT IDEA

Cover a divan base with strong furnishing fabric to match your room scheme. Use a staple gun to fix it to the underside of the base. This is a tailored alternative to a loose valance.

scale: 1 square = 1 metre

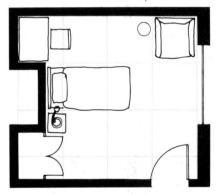

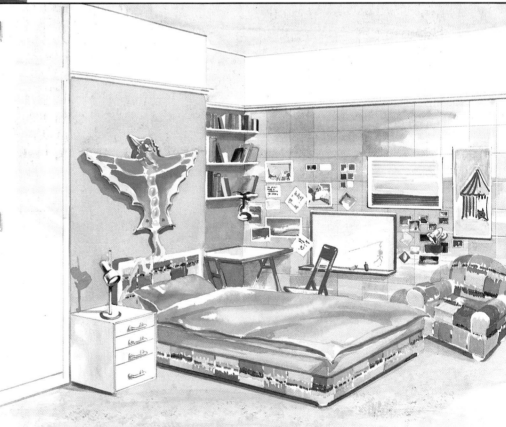

CLEVER BED ARRANGEMENTS

In most households with two or more children, bedrooms have to be shared. Even if the room is large, bunks may still be the best option where the room is used by both occupants for playing, reading and working, as well as for sleeping.

▷ *Off the floor*

There may seem no point in bunk beds if a room is for the exclusive use of one child, but there are advantages with an arrangement like this one. Here, bed, wardrobe, desk and bookcase take up the floor space of a single bed. This is a great plus in a small room, and leaves space for spreading out or, in a slightly bigger one, for a second bed.

▽ *Thinking of sharing*

Here the table is big enough for two to use at once, alternatively there is ample space for one child to be playing on the floor while the other is working or curled up on the settee reading a book.

The tubular metal furniture and clear colours chosen for this otherwise plain room help create an illusion of even greater space.

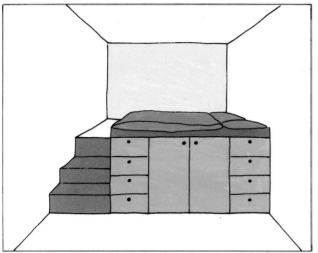

◁ **A sleeping platform**
Built on top of cupboards and chests-of-drawers, this is an ideal space-saving idea for an older child. There are carpeted steps up the side to the bed.

▽ **Wardrobe storage**
The sturdy cupboard door, with strong hinges, carries rungs to make a ladder. Additional shelving is arranged behind and along the bunks.

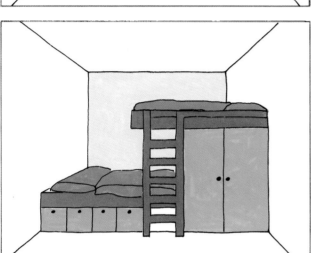

△ **An overlapping set-up**
For a room that is not wide enough to take two beds foot to foot, this system provides two sleeping platforms as well as a wardrobe and under-bed storage.

▷ **Strong metal framework**
A system of bunks, access ladder and shelving using scaffolding. An idea for the sure-footed only. (It is essential to make sure heads can't get stuck between bars.)

◁ **Bed-sit**
Low platform-based beds set at right angles to one another create a cosy corner for sleeping or idling. Quilted fitted covers give the neat look of a tailored sofa and lots of cushions add to the comfort.

An all-over scheme of blue and white mini-print paper and fabric gives a more spacious feel. Accents of pattern and colour come from the appliqué hanging, cushions and patchwork quilts.

The beds are rather close for more than one child for general use but are fun for sharing with an occasional visitor.

67

▷ **Occasional guest**

Most children love having friends to stay the night, but with a small room like this attic, a sociable soul has a problem. One answer is to choose a space-saving trundle bed like this one with another underneath which pulls out easily when it is needed. When not in use, it tucks neatly away to leave valuable play space.

◁ **Toy tidy**

There should be no arguments about putting away toys at night in this household; they are all simply pushed out of sight behind this cheerful threefold screen. During the day it makes a splendid display board or play house. It is simple to make and fun to decorate – with a painted scene or images cut out from a border or frieze and protected with several coats of polyurethane which can be easily wiped clean.

▷ **Book store**

A neat way to house books and oddments is by building plenty of shallow shelves beside and above the doorway, using those higher up for less favourite ones and for display. In this room the built-in cupboard finishes short of the doorway and this space would otherwise have been wasted.

Interest is added by outlining the cupboard mouldings with a colour from the wallpaper border and cutting out motifs to decorate the top door panels.

TEENAGERS' ROOMS: 12 to 17 YEARS

Teenagers' rooms require a delicate compromise between parental wishes and the need for self-expression.

Clichés and anecdotes on the subject abound, but the irrefutable fact is that teenagers *are* messy, noisy and disruptive when it comes to fitting into the family home. Coping with 12- to 17-year-olds almost always requires forethought, co-operation and, above all, patience.

Try to anticipate the future. Make changes before they are forced on you and reach decisions together with your teenagers to prevent avoidable opposition to parental wishes.

Above all, remember that your teenagers are approaching adulthood and, quite rightly, want privacy and the opportunity to express themselves in their own way (even if their taste isn't yours). It is up to the adults to arrange matters discreetly so as to achieve peace and equilibrium.

So plan, as you must do with every room in your home. Your teenagers will want to entertain. Is this to be in their own rooms, or are you (and they) willing to share the living room with their friends? Where is homework to be done? It is only fair to them to provide a quiet workspace. Is modern music popular with all the family, or do you want it kept out of earshot?

Begin by studying your options. Perhaps children have shared a bedroom in the past and are now clamouring for individual rooms. Can this be done? Would a loft or garage conversion provide additional accommodation? Can you site the teenage rooms away from the living areas and master bedroom to minimize noise distraction?

Practical yet individual
Two tall shelving units, which include a folding table, flank a desk in this study/bedroom. The wooden furniture and plain walls set off the strongly-patterned furnishings.

△ **Flexible and colourful**
Brightly-coloured accessories and furnishings add youthfulness to a basically plain, pale-coloured room. A sag bag and several large, firm cushions covered in geometric designs provide flexible and comfortable seating for youngsters.

The storage is inconspicuous – a wicker basket topped by a cushion, drawers beneath the raised bed, and a chest of drawers in one alcove. A long worktop fixed to the wall acts as a desk.

BRIGHT IDEA

A practical desk is essential equipment in any teenager's room. The table legs on the improvised desk shown here also provide storage space – the result is both practical and stylish. A length of hardwearing kitchen worktop sits on top of neat plastic-coated wire stacking units. The pull-out baskets provide ample storage space for writing equipment, files, papers and books and the matching chair can be folded away when not in use.

Trestles or filing cabinets can be used in a similar way. (Old and scratched filing cabinets can be rejuvenated with a coat of brightly-coloured spray-paint.)

A MULTI-FUNCTIONAL ROOM

A teenager's room is more than a bedroom. It is also a living room and study, and so needs to be furnished with an eye to flexibility.

A bed occupies a large area and will accumulate junk during the day. For small rooms, look at beds which are designed so that the space above or below can be put to practical use. Sofa or folding beds aren't necessarily the best choice – how many teenagers actually make their bed each morning? Beds which sit on a desk or clothes storage unit may be better.

Chairs must be able to withstand the punishment meted out by teenagers. Bean bags or large floor cushions are modern in image, and perfect for lounging on. The divan bed comes into

its own by doubling as a seat for more than one.

A desk All teenagers need encouragement to study and a desk with good lighting and storage is essential. If you have to house a computer, a separate worktop is advisable. Otherwise, the desk is cluttered with computer paraphernalia and study suffers. Don't forget that discs, tapes and other software need a safe home where they won't be bent, buried, or trodden on.

Hi-fi equipment can be very compact these days, and is almost bound to be an essential element of every teenager's room. Wall-mounting saves floor space and many units are designed to be stacked. Try to position the sound gear within cable length of seating to encourage the use of headphones!

△ *A teenage hideaway*
Self-assembly furniture systems are available in many different formats. The one used in this teenager's room incorporates a desk and small storage drawers below a bunk bed. Alternative arrangements include sofa or cupboard as well as sleeping and working space.

Storage If you are to win the battle for tidiness, allow adequate space for all the cherished bits and pieces which can *never* be thrown away, as well as clothes and books. Old-fashioned trunks look good (and trendy), can double as seating, and are capacious. Fit the largest wardrobe or chest of drawers that money and space will allow. When you insist on a clean-up at least there will be somewhere for everything to go.

◁ *Stylish co-ordination*
This girl's room is practical as well as charming. The pretty wallpaper co-ordinates with the fabric used for the blinds, curtains, bedcovering and cushions to create a unified look.

The natural wooden shelf which runs under the window and around the bed provides bedside storage, while trundle beds mean that a friend can stay for the night with the minimum of disruption.

▽ *Hobby area*
Wherever possible, it's worth encouraging teenagers' hobbies by providing a quiet corner where they can be pursued. This youngster is able to develop his interest in chemistry and computers with ample working space and deep shelves fitted into an alcove.

HARD-WEARING DECOR

The furnishings, floor and wallcoverings used in any teenager's room need to be robust as well as providing a neutral background for changing tastes.

Soundproofing from the noise of voices as well as the radio and hi-fi is important. If teenagers gather to chat late at night next door to the master bedroom everyone suffers; they because they know you can hear, you because you can! Replacing hollow doors with solid ones or lining a wall with books considerably reduces noise levels.

Walls Paint is the best wallcovering, simply because it can be easily renewed to keep up with changing fashions. A metre-wide roll of cork can run the length of an entire wall. It makes an ideal display board for everything from post-

ers to reminder notes and coveted certificates and is easily fixed to the wall. Such a noticeboard also helps to reduce noise levels.

Floors must be able to take punishment. Standard domestic carpet, unless of the highest quality, may quickly look tawdry. Contract carpet used in offices is longlasting, easily cleaned and not too hard underfoot. Polished floorboards with scatter rugs are attractive, but not if the teenager's room is directly above a room where you want peace and quiet. Cork tiles and lino are practical, hardwearing and attractive.

Coir matting is often recommended as a cheap, durable floorcovering, but beware! It harbours dust and even the most powerful cleaner will have difficulty lifting the accumulated dirt, necessitating complete removal periodically.

△ Flexibility
Freestanding furniture is easily rearranged to create a brand new layout to meet changing needs. This style of furniture would suit almost any bedroom – the room is given an individual character by means of cheerful accessories and paintings, and a duvet cover whose bold stripes are echoed in the stripes of the venetian blind.

▷ Nostalgia
This bedroom has been made intensely personal simply by draping several pendant lamps with cloths edged in pretty scallops. In addition, the noticeboard is crammed with an ever-growing collection of postcards and mementos. The walls and furniture are painted in pale tones to create a restful background.

◁ *Black and white fantasy*
The 'shell' of this room has been kept simple so that the style can be altered without embarking on a major redecoration project.

Its stunning atmosphere stems almost entirely from the creative use of black paint (on the chair and floor), black and white soft furnishings (such as the bedlinen and austrian blind) and black and white accessories (including the dress hanging on the wall).

▽ *Dramatic contrasts*
This study corner largely depends for its stylishness on dramatic colours and modern, hardwearing furniture.

The glossy black tabletop matches both the up-to-date rubber stud flooring, the desk lamp and the painted bookshelves. Splashes of orange and pineapple yellow are picked out in the relief wallpaper and the edges of the shelves and tabletop for a stunning contrast.

TEENAGERS' CHOICE

Teenagers have notoriously strong and independent views on good and bad taste. While persuasion may work in many instances, you may feel you have to put your foot down on certain subjects – the choice of expensive carpet, for example. Where changes can be more easily made, though, it's often best to give youngsters a free hand. After all, trial and error is one of the best ways of learning.

The colour scheme, for example, may be one area which demands compromise. Striking colours are all very well today, but what happens when they fall out of favour? Covering over strong tones calls for hard work and expense, since several coats of paint will be necessary. So although the choice of colours really should be up to the teenagers, encourage them to stop and think for a moment before setting to work with a paintbrush.

Similarly, accessories, furnishings and bedlinen are cheaper than pieces of furniture and so can be more easily changed when they fall out of favour.

A combination of patience, persuasion and tolerance should result in a workable compromise.

A YOUNG PERSON'S BEDSITTING ROOM

A young adult needs space to develop an independent lifestyle within the family home.

There comes a time in a young person's life when the chance to take steps towards independence is welcomed. At the late or post-teen stage, young people need space to run their own lives, with the family at hand for support if necessary. A bedsitting room within the family home will give a student or first jobber the privacy needed for self-sufficient living.

Negotiation with your son or daughter will be necessary, as a young person won't appreciate being presented with a *fait accompli.* Taste at this age is likely to be more sophisticated than in the early teens, though some tactful steering away from stylistic extremes may be necessary if the space is to be easily reclaimed once the occupier has moved out. But a mutual respect is important. A first jobber may well want to supply some witty details as personal finishing touches or even make a financial contribution to the decorating cost.

△ *Great divide*

A combined sleeping and living quarter needs careful thinking through if it's to produce a workable whole. A divider can be used to separate different functions in a room. This one successfully closes off the sleeping area while open sections give an impression of space and provide shelving for an attractive display.

SETTING THE SCENE

To encourage a sense of independence, the bedsitting room should ideally be at a remove from the rest of the family. Attic rooms are often a good shape for one-room living; the garret ambience will doubtless be relished, and young legs can take stairs in their stride. For a room that is some distance from communal quarters, you may want some form of communication, such as a bell, to keep in touch. If the accommodation is within the family complex, it should be a no-go area for younger brothers and sisters.

Conventional furnishing may not be necessary or appropriate. Keep the overall design simple. The young person will of course be responsible for tidying and cleaning the room, and uncluttered lines will help to encourage good practice.

To live, sleep and eat in a small area requires skilful planning. Consider a versatile sleeping/seating arrangement, such as a futon which can be rolled or folded to form daytime seating. Fold-up or pull-down beds may make the most of a tight space, or a divan bed with storage under could have huge cushions for additional seating when friends are in. For a high-ceilinged room a more ambitious project to save floor space could include a tubular platform bed with storage below the raised sleeping arrangement.

SELF-SUFFICIENT LIVING

Though the occupant will probably be putting in frequent appearances at mealtimes to eat with the family, separate catering facilities will help encourage self sufficiency. Equipment could range from a basic hotplate and kettle for snacks and hot drinks to a complete mini-kitchen, screened or curtained from view.

Provision of a separate bath or shower would be ideal. There is a range of tiny bathrooms and fold-away showers on the market which would take up little space in a multi-purpose room. And an extra shower or bathroom would certainly prove useful once the bedsitter has been vacated. If the provision of separate facilities is not possible, and the youngster has to share the family bathroom, try at least to provide a wash basin in the bedsitting room.

Your young son or daughter is likely to be a more civilized being than during the early teenage years, but sidestep possible conflict through anticipation of problem areas. Lay down strict house rules regarding noise levels from the very beginning. A well-fitting, draught-proofed door, thick curtaining, wall-to-wall carpets and insulating mats on electronic equipment will all help to deaden unwelcome sound. Music fans should be encouraged to use earphones when the family wants peace and quiet, as the base element is not contained by the usual sound-deadening properties of fitted carpets, bookshelves and soft furnishings.

Expensive wall finishes may not be appropriate, particularly if posters or theatre programmes are likely to be stuck to the wall. Choose a satin-finish oil-based paint for the greatest resistance to damage.

▽ *Designs on space*
Storage is a critical factor in a multi-purpose room. A vast built-in wardrobe is one of the cheapest ways to provide cupboard storage, and can also be used as a dressing room. By painting furniture and walls in the same muted tones, the room is given a measure of co-ordinated restraint.

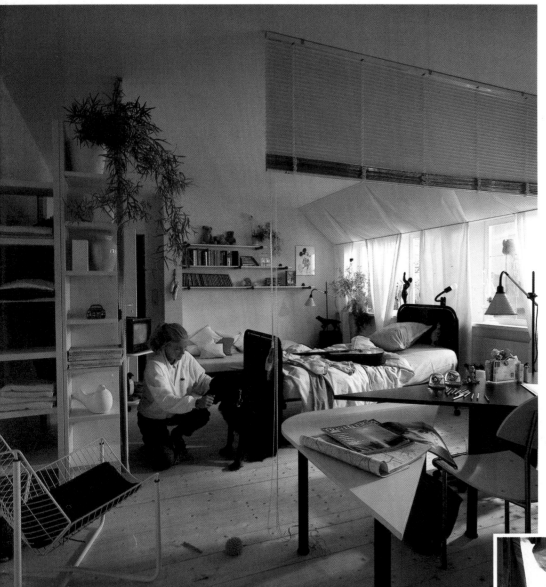

STOWING THE GEAR

Finding the best way of organizing storage of possessions in a bedsitting room is quite a challenge. Even if the lifestyle is casual, a sense of order is important, or informality can collapse into chaos. Plan an overall storage system from the start, so that floor space isn't crowded with bits and pieces all housed separately.

Look first at the layout, and consider how the room is likely to be used. Discuss the possibility of establishing areas for different functions – living, sleeping, catering – and plan the storage accordingly. If space is tight, you could gather together everything that needs to be stored in a large, walk-in cupboard.

Adjustable shelving can be inexpensive; open shelves are useful for books, hi-fi equipment and ornaments, and you could screen off a section to hold less sightly goods. Wire systems with hanging space for clothes provide inexpensive storage.

Modular units are a flexible choice for one-room living as they can be built up along a wall or used as freestanding dividers. The young person could investigate innovative storage, such as the tough, workmanlike units featured in the catalogues of firms supplying fitments for hospitals, shops and offices. For example, filing cabinets are now available in vibrant colours. A small cabinet could be used as a bedside table, while two or three larger models, holding general possessions, could serve as a room divider. House heavier belongings in lower drawers to keep cabinets stable.

▷ **Futon flexibility**
A futon is a versatile choice for one-room living, and is often popular with the young who relish an informal and unconventional approach to furnishing. A blanket box or old pine chest could be used for storing bedding during the day, and double as an occasional or bedside table.

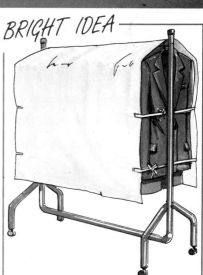

BRIGHT IDEA

Clothes cover-up A wardrobe is often too large and cumbersome a piece of furniture to fit easily into a multi-purpose room. A flexible and inexpensive alternative is to use a hanging rail, such as those found in clothes shops. To protect the clothes from dust and give a neat finish, drape a loose cover over the stored garments, and secure the open ends with ties.

△ Colour galore

This brilliant extravaganza of colour and pattern has been put together with tremendous verve and conviction. Careful use of blue throughout calms a blaze of colour. The room includes a wealth of imaginative detail that a young person could use to good effect – old furniture can be covered in handsome fabrics, and painted floor tiles and garden chairs can match the overall scheme. The room joyfully reflects the exuberance of youth, but definitely isn't for the faint-hearted.

▷ Self sufficiency

The complete mini-kitchen: occupying a space of only 600mm by 1000mm, the unit incorporates a sink with drainer, two-ring hob, small refrigerator and cupboard for storage. For more ambitious catering, consider fitting a multi-function microwave to the wall above the unit. The whole ensemble could be neatly screened from the rest of the bedsitting room.

FINDING SPACE FOR A PARENT

An elderly person needs privacy to live in dignity and comfort within the family home.

There can come a time when, for peace of mind, the decision is taken to have an elderly parent move in to make a home with you. There are blessings all round, but difficulties will also have to be faced. To be thrust suddenly into the noisy bustle of family life can mean a major adjustment for an elderly person; the family also will have to face changes in routine and new living arrangements.

It's important that the elderly are encouraged to remain active and deal with everyday tasks for themselves; this will make it easier for you, but your parent must be provided with the means for independent living. Even if the elderly person is fit, stairs may cause problems in the future, so conversion of a downstairs study or dining room would be ideal. If there is no bathroom, consider installing at least a lavatory and wash basin.

If losing a room puts pressure on the rest of the house and you cannot get by with doubling up – perhaps with two children sharing a room, or combining living and dining rooms – you may need to contemplate more substantial structural alterations. Could the loft or basement be converted to make extra rooms for the family? Would a garage conversion or single-storey extension create a suitable separate annexe?

Once these major issues have been resolved, consider the important aspect of safety. An intercom system or panic button can connect with the main household in case of emergency. A separate telephone is a good idea; systems that give visual signals help the hard of hearing. If stairs cannot be avoided, provide good lighting and sturdy handrails.

Finally, remember the little touches that will make your parent feel cherished – try to give them a room with a pleasant view, and provide pot plants and perhaps even a window box for green fingers to set to work on.

Cosy comfort
In this pretty scheme folding louvre doors conceal clothes and other possessions, and can also seal off the kitchen area which is just a step away. Attention to detail will ease an older person's life: well-sited lights illuminate key points, tables keep requirements within reach and a footstool can rest weary legs or provide extra seating when grandchildren drop in for a chat. Pretty chintz and pot plants make it all seem just like home.

SELF-SUFFICIENT CATERING

Even if Grandmother or Grandad will be joining the family for most meals, supply some basic provision for making hot drinks and light snacks. For a small kitchen area with self-sufficient possibilities look for a worktop cooker or multi-function microwave for cooking hot meals or reheating dishes from your freezer.

If an able-bodied elderly person wants greater independence, the cooking facilities could extend – space permitting – to a complete mini kitchen, which could either be custom built or assembled more cheaply yourself.

A small adjoining room would be ideal for separate catering. But if the equipment has to be within the living area find the most unobtrusive location – in an alcove, perhaps, or in a neat line along one wall. Storage should be accessible, with nothing too high or low; consider pull-out carousel units, or drawers. Check that everything is as stable as possible, with no protruding sharp edges.

Touch controls or big rocker switches, and quarter-turn lever taps for the sink, are easiest for frail fingers. If a gas cooker is to be used, a flame-failure device is a good safety measure: the gas supply is cut off if the flame blows out or fails to ignite for any reason.

△ *A peaceful retreat*
Away from the bustle of family life, a pleasant room for peaceful relaxation in a beloved old armchair, with the small kitchen nicely convenient. Beside the glowing fire is space for photographs and treasured mementoes.

▽ *Compact catering*
A neat, ready-made kitchen containing all the essentials for self-sufficient catering. After use, the kitchen is concealed behind bi-fold wooden doors which are good-looking enough to blend with sitting room decoration.

SITTING PRETTY

More than just a place for sleep, a room for an elderly person should be designed for normal activities – reading, watching television and having family and friends drop in.

Built-in storage for clothes and other possessions may work better than several large pieces of furniture. The bed should not be dominant – perhaps a divan with day cover – but site it so that bedmaking isn't awkward. Sofa beds save space but need making up every evening, and the muscle power needed to operate the mechanism may be beyond an older person.

Seating should not be too soft, or low, making it difficult to rise from. Look at chairs specifically designed for the elderly, or choose a wing chair with footrest to give support.

Choose good general lighting and concentrated light for close work. Wall lights by the bed will avoid the danger of confusion in the dark.

Warmth is vital. The room could be connected to the central heating system, with extra topping up from a safe appliance. Open or radiant fires can be a real danger: if they must be used, fit a guard and don't place objects that may be needed on the mantelpiece above the fire.

▽ **Room to relax**
Though it does not dominate the room, which remains essentially a living area, this bed has been sited for easy access. A fitted cover can be pulled over in the morning, and the bed used for additional seating when friends drop in, or for daytime naps.

△ **Home comforts**
In this alternative arrangement an orthopaedic armchair gives support, and the desk is near the window for good light and a pleasant view. Blinds have been replaced by the more traditional net for privacy and thick curtaining to keep the room cosily snug.

A PERSONAL AFFAIR

An elderly person needs well-lit, easy access to bathroom facilities, day and night. Whether you are adapting an existing bathroom or planning a new one, safety must be a prime concern.

Ensure you can get into the bathroom to give assistance if there should be a mishap; fit a lock with an emergency safety device, or attach a sign which will indicate occupancy to give privacy without the need for a lock.

The floor should be non-slip, particularly in areas which may get wet. A fitted carpet suitable for bathroom use is warm and comfortable underfoot, and eliminates the necessity for mats that can ruck dangerously.

There should be plenty of well-placed hand holds, for example around the lavatory if the relative is infirm, and grab rails on the bath. Non-standard baths are available if space is limited, and both shower and bath should have non-slip mats.

If a shower is to be installed, safety must again be a priority: a fold-down seat for showering or – installed outside the cubicle – a safe resting place for drying and dressing. As in the kitchen, quarter-turn lever taps give even arthritic fingers easy control of water for sink or bath.

If the new resident is to share the family bathroom, you may have to install safety features to meet the special needs of the elderly. Access to the bathroom should be lit at night, and the rest of the family must take care over leaving the room utterly safe.

△ Compact bathroom
If you have the space, an elderly person would enjoy relaxing in a warm bath in the comfort of a compact, en suite bathroom. Note the handrails to ease getting into and out of the bath, and the non-slip base. Toiletries are kept within easy reach in open shelves above the hand basin.

▽ Private convenience
Grab rails around this lavatory will give an infirm relative the confidence to attend to personal needs with a minimum of assistance.

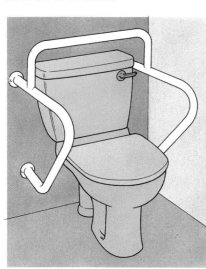

△ At ease
This easy-clean seat can fold down for a leisurely, safe shower. The height of the water spray can be adjusted on the slide bar for a sitting position. For a stand-up shower the seat folds neatly out of the way. A non-slip mat is, of course, essential.

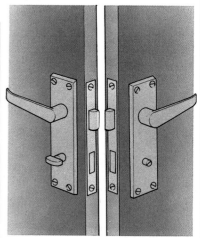

BEDS: MATTRESSES AND BASES

There are many different types of mattresses and bases available. It is important to choose the right combination.

This chapter looks at the essential parts of a bed – mattress and base. The following chapter looks at the different sorts of beds available. A base can be an integral part of the bed frame, such as a wire-sprung base on a brass bed or a wooden slatted base on a wooden bed, but today most beds are divan beds where the base comes with a mattress.

Try to buy your mattress with the base – this is possible with a divan bed. If you want a new mattress for a brass or wooden framed bed, seek advice.

MATTRESS INTERIORS

It is important to find out what is inside a mattress, as this determines its quality and how comfortable it is likely to be. Most mattresses available today divide into two basic groups: those with sprung interiors and those which are filled with foam.

Foam Most foam mattresses are a combination of latex foam, a natural rubber and relatively soft, and synthetic foam which tends to be much firmer. You can also get mattresses made from one or the other.

Sprung There are a variety of different types available. The firmness of the mattress depends mainly on the thickness of the wire used for the springs and how many there are. The label on the mattress should state how many springs it contains. (Expect 500 in the cheapest double size, and over 1,000 in a top-quality one.)

FOAM

Style The cheapest sort of foam mattress is the single foam slab which is simply slotted into a mattress cover. The firmer the foam is, the more likely it is to be synthetic, the softer it is, the more likely it is to be a latex foam.

In use Avoid this type of mattress if you intend to sleep on it each night as it is really only adequate for an occasional bed.

Watchpoint The foam should be at least 10cm thick if it is to be at all comfortable.

MIXED FOAM

Style This mattress is made up of at least two layers of foam; a bottom layer of firm foam (probably synthetic such as polyurethane or polyether foam) and a soft top layer (latex foam, for example). This combination should give sufficient support and solidity, as well as a surface

which moulds into the contours of the body. Some manufacturers also mould the foam into a honeycomb formulation, for example, to give it varying degress of softness or firmness.

In use Foam doesn't harbour dust, so is non-allergenic. It's also light and easy to lift.

Watchpoint Most sit in a sunken wooden bed frame. Make sure the mattress is thick enough to be higher than the wooden sides – if not you end up lying on them.

FOAM WITH INSET SPRINGS

Style This type is made from a solid block of foam with holes punched in it to take open coil springs.

In use It has the 'give' of a sprung mattress (see below), but is much cheaper.

Watchpoint Make sure there is plenty of padding over the foam, so the springs don't poke through.

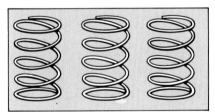

△ **OPEN SPRINGS**

Style Most of the less expensive mattresses are open-sprung; simple, open, upright, coil springs clipped together at the top and the bottom within a wire mesh framework in the mattress.

In use The springs move as one unit. They can then be upholstered with hair (on more expensive types) and/or layers of padding.

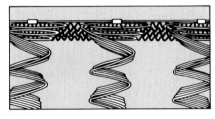

△ **CONTINUOUS SPRINGS**

Style This is a continuous length of wire 'knitted' together to produce a web effect, held in place by a wire framework inside the mattress.

In use This mattress moves and wears in much the same way as an open-sprung type.

Watchpoint Try out both open and continuous spring mattresses to find out which suits you best.

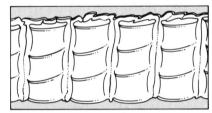

△ **POCKETED SPRINGS**

Style This mattress, where each spring is hand-sewn under tension into its own pocket, is the most expensive type.

In use Each spring works on its own (independent of its neighbour) to support the body.

Watchpoint The greater the number of springs, the better the mattress is likely to be.

UPHOLSTERY

Never buy a mattress on looks alone. A pretty cover is soon hidden under the bedclothes.

Ticking The mattress cover is known as the ticking. It can be made of natural fibres such as cotton or synthetics such as rayon. It is said that natural fibres allow the mattress to 'breathe' more efficiently than synthetic fibres. The latter tend to give the ticking a smooth, slippery surface, from which bedcovers are prone to slip.

Padding Directly under the ticking are layers of padding which can be made up of felt, coir or even wool. This adds warmth and comfort.

Stitching The stitching on top of the mattress which appears to give a pretty patterned effect actually holds the mattress cover to the padding.

Tufting A mattress can be finished off with buttons or what looks like cotton or felt washers. This is done by hand and found on good quality mattresses giving them a dimpled effect. The mattress is punched through with tapes which are held in place with washers or buttons.

Smooth tops are found on the very cheapest mattresses. The cover has simply been pulled tightly over the mattress.

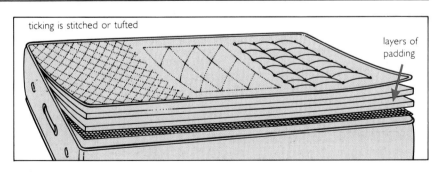

ticking is stitched or tufted

layers of padding

BED SIZES	Metric	Imperial
Small single	90×190cm	3ft×6ft 3in
Standard single	100×200cm	3ft 3in×6ft 7in
Small double	135×190cm	4ft 6in×6ft 3in
Standard double	150×200cm	5ft×6ft 7in

These are the only four standard British bed sizes. Beds bigger than a standard double are King or Queen sizes, but these aren't standardized, and can vary from one manufacturer to manufacturer so ask for advice.

BED BASES

Traditionally the bed base was incorporated into the bed frame, also known as the bedstead. But these days the most popular bed is the divan which consists of mattress and separate base.
Divan bases The base is usually the same shape and roughly the same size as its mattress and both are sold together as one unit. They are usually covered in the same fabric too. However, there are different ways in which the base – as well as the mattress – can be made, (see below).
Other bases such as wooden slatted and metal bases are an in-built part of the bed frame (or bedstead) and are made up of a headboard, footboard and base all in one. The type of bed you choose automatically gives you a certain type of base. So a wooden framed bed usually has a wooden head- and footboard and a slatted base and a metal bedstead has a metal head- and footboard and either a plain wire mesh or open sprung base (see below).

There are no hard and fast rules as to which one type of bed base is the best, because to a large extent it depends on what you want.

DIVAN BASES

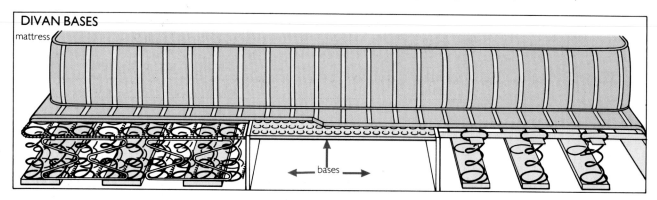

mattress

bases

△ SPRUNG-EDGE BASE
Style A wooden base supports an upholstered, open coil spring unit on top. It provides a fully sprung platform with springs right up to the edges.
In use The most expensive, luxurious base. It supports a mattress evenly across the surface.
Watchpoint It is usually 10cm deeper than other bases. Continual sitting on the edge of the bed can damage the springs, so it's not ideal for teenager's rooms where the bed is often used as seating.

△ SOLID TOP BASE
Style This base is not sprung but is just a wooden platform. Some types are also upholstered with foam or fibre to give extra comfort.
In use This is an extremely firm base and the accompanying mattress must be able to withstand the effect of the hardness.
Watchpoint There should be ventilation holes drilled in this type of base. If these are absent the mattress won't be able to breathe.

△ FIRM-EDGE BASE
Style Not as deep as the sprung-edge base. The springs are kept firmly in position with webbing strung from side to side and top to bottom. All this is then held within a wooden frame (ie. boxed in), which is why it is called firm-edge.
In use Because of the firm edge, this base can eventually 'give' in the centre producing a dip.
Watchpoint If you are short of space look for firm-edge bases which have built-in storage areas.

OTHER BASES

▷ SLATTED WOOD BASE
Style This base is made up from flat pieces of wood held on two side support rails. The slats may be screwed into place individually or stapled on to lengths of webbing which are laid on the support rails. The width of the slats and the distance between them are variable.
In use This firm base is found on most wooden framed beds and most children's beds.
Watchpoint Always buy the correct mattress; the wrong sort could sag between the slats.

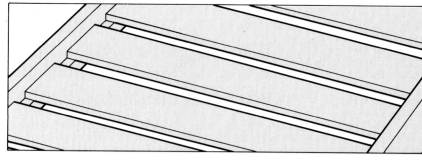

▷ HORIZONTAL SPRUNG BASE
Style This is a more luxurious metal base than the simple horizontal wire mesh base found on older style brass beds, for example. A horizontal sprung base consists of a layer of thick metal mesh with open springing in it. It spans the area between a metal head- and footboard and side rails.
In use Firmer than the traditional divan and more resilient than either a slatted or solid base.
Watchpoint This type of bed can be sold without a mattress, take advice from your retailer when choosing one to go with it.

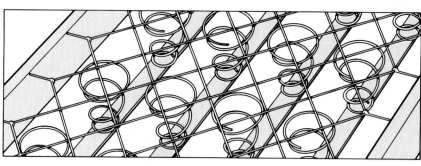

▷ ADJUSTABLE DIVAN BASE
Style There are some divan bases on the market which are adjustable.
In use Both ends of the bed can be raised by altering the controls. Raising the foot end allows you to lie with your feet up and raising the head end means you can sit up in bed or get in and out of bed with more ease.

▷▷ ADJUSTABLE WOODEN SLATTED BASE
Style Wooden slats sit across a box-like frame to form the base of the bed.
In use Both ends of the bed can be adjusted manually or mechanically (optional extra).
Watchpoint This base is available as a single or double bed. The double bed is made up of two separately adjustable bases.

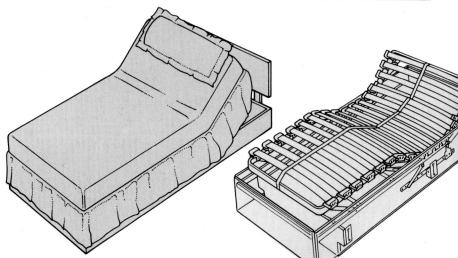

DIFFERENT TYPES OF BED

Beds come in all shapes, sizes and styles. Choose a type which suits you, your partner and the bedroom furnishings.

On average a third of your life is spent in bed. This fact alone surely makes your bed the most important piece of furniture in the bedroom.

Buying new An average mattress is at its best for only 10-15 years. So if you have a divan bed which is older than this the mattress and the base probably needs replacing. (Remember that a firm-edge or sprung-edge divan base tends to take on the same faults as the mattress.) If you have a wooden framed bed with a slatted base or a metal framed bed with a wire sprung base after 10-15 years you will need to renew only the mattress as these bases are resilient.

Which bed? As explained in the previous chapter all beds are made up of two basic parts – base and mattress. This chapter looks at different types of bed. The first section looks at the divan bed which consists of a mattress and base without a frame, plus a headboard which is usually sold as an additional extra. The second section looks at traditional bedsteads – base, head- and footboard all joined together. The third section covers space-saving beds which have a unique framework so they double up as storage or can be stowed away.

CHECKLIST
Before you choose your bed think carefully about your requirements.
- [ ] Who is the bed for – adult or child?
- [ ] How often is it likely to be used? Beds that are slept in every night must be more substantial than those used only occasionally.
- [ ] The only way to test a bed properly is to lie down on it.
- [ ] When lying flat out on the bed can you slide your hand easily into the small of your back? If you can the bed may be too hard, but if you can't it may be too soft. If the bed fills the gap in the small of your back, but you can still squeeze in your hand, the bed is giving you the right sort of support.
- [ ] Turn on your side. If this is difficult the bed is too soft.
- [ ] Ask sales people about the construction and upholstery.

DIVAN BEDS

Style A divan bed is made up of a base and mattress. It can be bought in sizes ranging from a small single to a Supersize (which is 210 × 210cm). The bases for all double-sized divan beds are made in two pieces and hinged together so they can be folded in two for transporting or manoeuvring through doorways. Alternatively, you can buy a double divan which consists of two linked-up single bases and two single mattresses zipped together.

In use This type of double divan (made up of two single mattresses and bases) is practical if there is a big difference between your weight and your partner's. Divan bases should have a standard fixing for a headboard to be attached. Also, there are many divan bases available (sprung or unsprung) which have drawer storage.

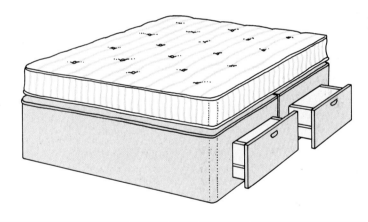

HEADBOARDS

A headboard should protect the wall behind the bed from getting dirty and also provide a relatively comfortable surface to rest against.

Padded headboards are made up of a wooden board covered in fabric (usually a velvet-like fabric), which sandwiches layers of padding. Look out for types with removable covers.

Headrest set Bought as a set or can be put together separately yourself. A pole is attached to the wall above the bed from which cushions hang.

Metal headboards are generally purely decorative items because they are usually uncomfortable to lean against. They do, however, protect the wall.

Open cane headboards come in a variety of different designs and styles, painted or natural.

Woven cane headboards are more comfortable than open cane and therefore more popular. A wooden frame is filled with a woven cane middle which is springy and supportive for leaning against.

Wooden headboards can be solid pieces of wood or veneered wood (a thin layer of wood finish stuck on plywood or fibreboard). They can also be carved into decorative, open boards.

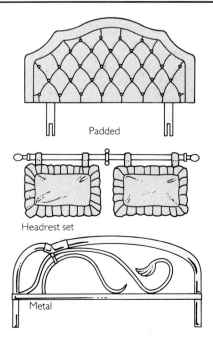

Padded

Headrest set

Metal

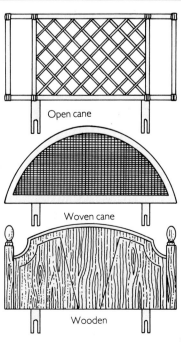

Open cane

Woven cane

Wooden

BEDSTEADS

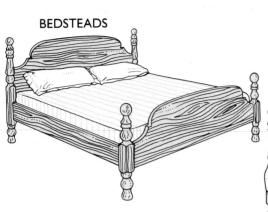

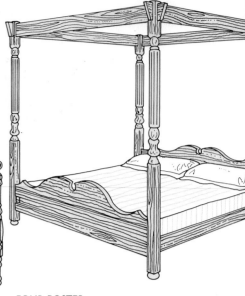

WOODEN COUNTRY STYLE
Style The bedstead is made of wood and the base is usually made up of wooden slats (see previous chapter).
In use Ensure joints are firmly fixed. Self-assembly beds fixed together with screws or clamps can become wobbly and squeaky after a time.

TRADITIONAL BRASS
Style Traditional brass bedsteads (or reproductions) are very popular. Most have a horizontal wire mesh or sprung base (see previous chapter).
In use Often quite high off the ground. Solid brass bedsteads are costly, brass-effect is cheaper.

FOUR-POSTER
Style Quite literally a bed with a post at each corner joined up to form a frame at the top over which a fabric canopy can be hung. (A bed without a top frame and canopy is called a pillar bed).
In use Designed to have side curtains around it.

SPACE-SAVERS

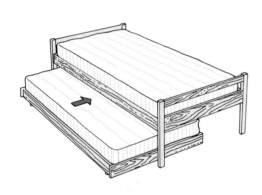

TRUNDLE
Style This single bed has a second bed with folding legs stored underneath it which can be pulled out when needed.
In use Use as two single beds or pushed together as a double. When the lower bed is raised make sure that it stands at the same height as the other bed.

Z-BED
Style A single folding bed with a thin mattress that is easy to store when not in use. Some have wooden head and base boards which can be used as a shelf when folded up.
In use Relatively cheap to buy but suitable for occasional use only.

FOLDAWAY
Style These beds are either hinged along one side or at one end so they can be folded (vertically or horizontally) flat against the wall.
In use The mechanism is locked into place against the wall so the bed can be concealed behind a curtain or inside a purpose-built cupboard.

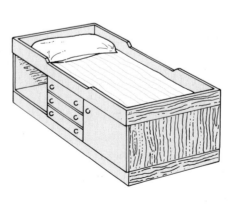

DOUBLE BUNK
Style One bed is set above the other. A ladder, which must be firmly fixed, gives access to top bunk.
In use It sleeps two children in the floor space of one. A safety rail should run along the top bunk.

STORAGE OR CABIN BUNK
Style This is a single bunk, but the bottom half is filled with drawers and drop-down cupboards.
In use Practical for children's bedrooms, but make sure your child can climb into bed easily.

SINGLE BUNK
Style Instead of two beds this houses a single bed.
In use The space underneath can have desk and drawers built in so it can be used as a study area or there are variations with seating areas.

CHOOSING BEDDING

Knowing what to look for and what is available when buying bedding could save you time and money.

It's easy to be confused by the large range of bedding in the shops. There are so many different colours and patterns in all shapes and sizes at different prices, so it helps to know what you want before buying.

The first half of this chapter looks at duvets and pillows and explains what fillings and methods of construction you can choose from. Overleaf, the second half looks at the selection of bedlinen available: sheets, pillowcases, valances and duvet covers.

DUVETS

Duvets or, as they are also called, continental quilts, are very popular for their lightness, warmth and convenience.

Warmth Body heat which is naturally given off by the sleeper, is trapped in the soft layers of the filling inside the case. The amount of warmth a duvet retains is graded in togs, roughly speaking, 2.5 togs is equal to the warmth of a standard wool blanket; 13.5 togs equal the warmth of five blankets (see table).

Quality and price is judged on the duvet filling and the case fabric, both of which should transmit (absorb and then evaporate) moisture vapour, because on average a person loses about half a litre of body moisture every night.

Size When buying a duvet choose a single duvet for a single bed and so on, But do measure your bed in case it is not a standard size. A duvet should be at least 46cm wider than the bed (see chart over page). For a double bed choose between one double duvet or two single duvets — one for each person.

TOG RATINGS

TOGS	4.5 6 7.5	9 10.5	12 13.5
WARMTH RATINGS	Summer use	Warm	Extra warm

Every duvet on sale should state its tog rating, so you can tell how warm it is. The higher the tog rating the better the insulating quality, which is what sustains the warmth. The tog ratings comply with the British Standard 5335.

DUVET FILLINGS

Fillings can be natural or synthetic.

Natural fillings available are down, down-and-feather, feather-and-down, feather, or less commonly, wool. Under British Standard 5335 there should be a minimum of 51 per cent of down in the down-and-feather mix and a minimum of 15 per cent of down in the feather-and-down mix.

The down (soft feathers) is usually duck down, but better quality down comes from the goose, and eiderdown is the ultimate duck down — extremely light and warm. All-down duvets are more expensive than other natural fillings and also cost more than quality synthetics, which compare with down-and-feather mixes.

Synthetic fillings are made of fine polyester fibres — the best of which are hollow like tubes. These hollow fibres are light with good insulating properties. Most good quality synthetic fillings are treated with silicone, so the fibres move freely creating a softer feel and 'loft'.

Loft is bulk in relation to weight — in other words fluffiness. This is desirable in all duvets because the more air there is in the filling, the better insulator it is likely to be. This is why eiderdown is superior to goose and ordinary duck, because it is fluffier and traps more air.

Warmth Double decker-style duvets fasten together for winter use and can be used as single units for summer. Two duvets together are not always as efficient as the sum of their togs might indicate, and also weigh more, so

separate duvets for winter and summer could be a better buy. Adjust temperature of natural fillings by shaking filling to bottom of the case on hot nights.

Washability Natural-filled duvets should usually be drycleaned. Synthetic-filled duvets are generally machine-washable.

PILLOW FILLINGS

Pillows, like duvets, can be filled with down, feathers (a combination of both) or polyester fibres. You can also buy foam-filled pillows (although these are now less common than previously).

Natural fillings Down makes the most luxurious filling, followed by a mixture of down-and-feather. Feather-and-down will be firmer. Curled poultry feathers are the cheapest filling, but tend to lose their curl and the ability to regain a plump, comfortable shape.

Foam Natural latex foam is springier than synthetic foam; avoid foam chips as these tend to become lumpy.

Synthetic Synthetic hollow fibres are springier than foam but neither are very snuggly. However, a recent development is a fluffy, down-like polyester filling composed of soft, tiny fibre balls — it is very acceptable and comfortable.

Sizes Unless pillows are marked 'special size', they should be of a standard size (approximately 48cm×74cm or 46cm×68cm) to fit most pillowcases on sale (don't forget that many European countries have very different shaped pillows — big and square). Choose soft-, medium- or firm-filled according to preference.

CHANNELS

As well as being stitched into a large case, duvet fillings are often also channelled lengthwise to keep them in place and stop them from becoming uneven and creating cold spots. Some natural fillings are simply contained in a case and move about freely, but this leads to an uneven distribution and cold spots. So, many different techniques of channeling have been developed.

Stitched-through channels are found mostly on natural fillings. Where top and bottom are sewn together cold spots can occur as insulation is at its thinnest.

Walled Cloth walls are sewn between the channels to help eliminate cold spots.

Step-stitched Here the channels are staggered in steps to eliminate cold spots.

Overlapped channels provide even thickness and should therefore eliminate cold spots.

Trapezium channels. Cloth walls are angled for a more even filling.

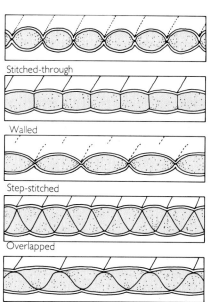

Stitched-through

Walled

Step-stitched

Overlapped

Trapezium

BED SIZE	FLAT SHEET SIZE	DUVET OR DUVET COVER SIZE
Small single 90cm×190cm (3ft×6ft 3in)	180cm×260cm (70in×102in)	140cm×200cm (55in×79in)
Standard single 100cm×200cm (3ft 3in×6ft 7in)	180cm×260cm (70in×102in)	140cm×200cm (55in×79in)
Small double 135cm×190cm (4ft 6in×6ft 3in)	230cm×260cm (90in×102in)	Two singles or: 200cm×200cm (79in×79in)
Standard double 150cm×200cm (5ft×6ft 7in)	230cm×275cm or 255cm×260cm (90in×108in) (100in×102in)	Two singles or: 230cm×250cm (90in×98in)
Queensize 165cm×200cm (5ft 6in×6ft 7in)	275cm×275cm (108in×108in)	Two singles or: 230cm×250cm (90in×98in)
Kingsize 183cm×200cm (6ft×6ft 7in)	305cm×320cm (120in×126in)	Two singles or: 250cm×300cm (98in×118in)

Sizes are approximate only and tend to vary from one manufacturer to another.

FABRIC FOR BEDLINEN

Bedlinen takes its name from the days when it was made of linen. Today sheets, pillowcases, duvet covers and valances come in a number of fabrics and finishes.

Linen is cool and strong, hardwearing, usually white and very expensive.

Cotton bedding is absorbent, soft and comfortable, but not as hardwearing as linen. What is called Swiss cotton is not Swiss, but usually an embroidered cotton. Egyptian cotton refers to a cotton made with long fine fibres – it is superior to ordinary cotton and more expensive. What is often called percale cotton refers to the thread – 180 fine threads per square inch – it makes a fine, delicate cotton.

A brushed fabric like cotton flannelette, has a soft, fibrous surface, is warm to touch – often bought as winter sheets.

Polyester/cotton mixes combine synthetic polyester with a proportion of cotton (usually 50:50 mix). They are non-shrink, hard-wearing and easy to launder, but not as soft as cotton.

Nylon bedding – smooth or brushed – is probably the least pleasant to sleep on. Pure nylon does not absorb moisture and can make you feel hot and clammy quickly. But it is easy to wash and dry.

Finishes An easy-care (or minimum care, minimum-iron) finish on cotton, for example, can make it less likely to crease. A stain-resistant treatment enables fibres to resist the absorption of stains.

SHEETS

There are three basic types of sheet.

Flat sheets are, as their name implies, the standard flat variety neatly finished at top and bottom and suitable as bottom and top sheets.

Fully-fitted sheets are for use as bottom sheets. They have four elasticated corners to fit closely over the mattress.

Semi-fitted sheets fit at the bottom of the bed, but are flat at the top. These are designed to be used as top sheets.

Sheets can be bought separately or in sets; usually available with matching or co-ordinating pillowcases or duvet covers. They are labelled double, single and so on, but always check sizes, allowing for a generous tuck-in for flat sheets. (A rule of thumb is bed width plus depth of the two sides to the floor – see chart.)

DUVET COVERS

The basic cover is a case or bag. It comes in many patterns or decorated with tucks, trims or borders. Some are padded and quilted to be used on their own during warmer summer nights. Duvets fit into covers through an end opening (or a side opening), fastened with poppers, ties or Velcro. Single-size covers may have an envelope opening.

VALANCES

A valance is a skirt (usually frilled or pleated, but can be plain), which is an attractive way to cover the base of a divan bed. It can also be used on other beds such as a wooden slatted or metal-framed bed – but may need to be adapted to fit round foot ends.

The under-mattress valance is put under the bed mattress. It is more difficult to fit than an over-mattress valance but unlikely to need frequent laundering. It allows use of both fitted or flat bottom sheets and top sheets.

The over-mattress valance is a sheet which combines a frilled skirt to cover the base and mattress all in one. But you can't tuck in a top sheet with this.

PILLOWCASES

Most pillowcases fit standard pillows, with an envelope opening deep enough to hold in the pillow securely. Often printed in patterns to match duvet covers or sheets, pillowcases may also be plain and/or finished with ribbon or embroidery.

Types Those with plain edges are described as 'housewife' style and flat bordered pillows, as 'Oxford', There are also fancy frilled pillowcases available and what is known as a pillow sham is a decorative day cover for a pillow.

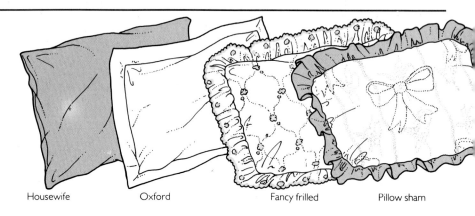

Housewife   Oxford   Fancy frilled   Pillow sham

WARDROBES

A wardrobe large enough to store shoes, hats and suitcases as well as clothes means less bedroom clutter.

Wardrobes can be divided into two main types, freestanding and fitted.

Freestanding wardrobes are either the conventional single piece of furniture with one, two or three doors, and those which can be placed in a line or run. The construction may be solid or self-assembly.

Fitted wardrobes can be custom-built, ready-made, assembled from kits or simply tracks with sliding or bi-fold doors. There are advantages and disadvantages to consider before deciding which type is most suitable for the bedrooms in your home.

WARDROBE INTERIORS

The interior can be fitted with full-length hanging, half-length hanging, drawers or shelves (which can be fixed, sliding or adjustable). Other features to look out for are a belt/tie rail, shoe rack, full-length or half-length mirror and top shelf. An interior light which comes on when the door is opened is also useful. See page 9 for advice on planning wardrobe storage.

FREESTANDING

Style Available with one, two or three doors in both traditional and modern styles; there is a greater variety in traditional designs. The hanging space can be full length or three-quarter length with a drawer or drawers beneath. Second-hand shops are a good place to find freestanding wardrobes. New wardrobes are usually sold with a matching range of furniture such as a dressing table, chest of drawers, bedside table and cheval mirror.

The pediment (top edge) and base plinth may be moulded, shaped or straight. Some wardrobes have rounded feet or even castors instead of a base plinth.

In use The most versatile type of wardrobe as it can be moved from room to room and house to house.

Watchpoints Do not make as economical use of space as fitted wardrobes. Can be solid construction or knockdown for self assembly. The former may be bulky and heavy to move – check the dimensions of the room and access up stairs and through doors before buying; the latter can be difficult to assemble single-handed.

A decorated pediment may restrict storage on top of the wardrobe and feet or a cut out base plinth with space underneath will allow dust to collect.

FREESTANDING IN A RUN

Style Although freestanding, these wardrobes are designed so that they can also be placed together to form a flush fitting run of cupboard units. Protruding side mouldings must be detachable on this type of wardrobe. Sometimes the whole top cornice is replaced by a single strip the length of the run.

Bridging units are available for some systems so that a chest of drawers or dressing table fitted at floor level between two full-length wardrobes can have high level cupboards fitted flush with the top. A bed may be incorporated between wardrobes in the same way.

In use These wardrobes are always sold as knockdown for self assembly so they can be dismantled and taken with you when you move.

Watchpoints If you are planning a run of freestanding wardrobes you must measure up the room very carefully. Some manufacturers offer a planning service free of charge. Check how versatile the interiors are. Can you alter the full-length

hanging to half-length, move shelves around, adjust their depth, etc?

As with single unit freestanding wardrobes, space may be wasted above and at the ends of the run of units as they probably won't fit a particular room exactly. Space can also be wasted at corners if the manufacturer does not include corner units in the range.

You will not be able to line up the wardrobe flush with the wall unless you are prepared to cut and remove the skirting board.

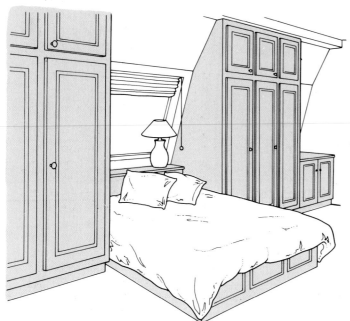

CUSTOM-BUILT FITTED UNITS

Style Floor-to-ceiling fitted units consisting of full-length hanging cupboards with top units above, bridging units and matching corner units, chests, dressing tables, bedside cabinets, etc. Some manufacturers offer additional features such as curved shelf end units and slide out mirrors. Designed and installed by the manufacturers to fit your room and storage requirements exactly.

The units are made from wood veneered (natural or painted) or plastic veneered particle board. The doors may be louvred, mirrored (partially or from floor to ceiling) decorated with moulding, left flush or hand painted.

In use The most efficient use of space as they can be tailored to fit a room perfectly. Every angle and feature, such as beams or sloping ceilings, are incorporated to make full use of space without leaving any dust traps. Check the interior can be redesigned at a later stage to suit changing needs. If space is a problem, bi-fold or sliding doors take up less room than do doors on hinges. These wardrobes are the most expensive and often incorporate unusual features such as swing out, high level hanging racks for easy access and touch sensitive interior lights.

Watchpoints Make sure the corner units are easily accessible and do not waste space. If you are having bridging units check that the base is well finished, particularly if they are over the bed. If your room has a decorative moulding, curtain rail or any other distinctive architectural feature, try to match these in the design of the units.

These are the most expensive type of wardrobe and because they are built to fit into a particular room, it is not possible to move them, but if designed well they do add to the value of your home.

READY-MADE FITTED UNITS

Style In appearance very similar to the custom-built fitted units but with a much larger range of designs and styles. They are put together using standard sizes of cupboards and drawers so they will not fit a given space exactly. In-fill panels are supplied to fill the spaces at the sides or top of a run of units and adjustable base units make up for any unevenness of the floor. These panels can be cut to fit round skirting boards, picture rails, etc. The more expensive ranges are usually designed for your room and installed by the manufacturer, which is inclusive in the price. The cheaper units are self assembly so plan and measure up the room before buying.

In use Check how versatile the interiors are — most ranges only allow for simple adjustments such as shelf depth.

Watchpoints Some units are fitted without backs which may make them cheaper but, if fitted to an outside wall can lead to problems with condensation. If the units have back panels check what they are made of. Veneered plywood fits better than thin veneered or painted hardboard which can warp.

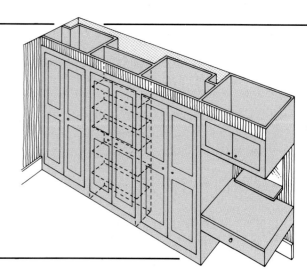

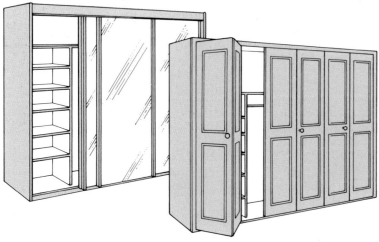

SLIDING/BI-FOLD DOORS

Style A track is fitted along the ceiling and/or the floor from wall to wall or from a wall to an end panel. Sliding or bi-fold doors are fitted or hung from the track. The doors may be full-length mirror panels, or wood/plastic veneer.

In use The interiors can be supplied by the manufacturer or you can design them yourself using wire stacking baskets. This system is ideal for rooms with sloping ceilings and the interior can be redesigned to suit changing needs.

Watchpoints The doors come in set heights so if you have very tall ceilings a filler piece attached to the ceiling joists has to be fitted. Some manufacturers will install the doors for you, others are self assembly.

KITS

Style Made up from a framework of uprights and shelves with the doors and side pieces fitted on to the framework after it has been built. Usually made from pine which is varnished or left natural.

In use As you build it yourself it is infinitely adjustable and can be dismantled and taken with you when you move.

Watchpoints Check for stability when building very large units. These may need to be fixed to the wall. Although versatile, once you have added up the cost of all the components it may not work out as cheap as some ready-made fitted wardrobe units.

BEDROOM FURNITURE

Consider your bedroom furniture carefully, for both looks and practicality.

Bedroom furniture is principally a means of storage, a neat and convenient way of keeping clothes, toiletries and sometimes luggage and study materials tidy, yet easily accessible. Looks are important as your chosen pieces will influence the whole style of your room, but shape and size must be carefully considered too. Often bedrooms are not large so you might have to be selective to ensure you get maximum storage in the minimum of space without losing out on good looks.

If space is very tight it might be worth considering fully fitted furniture. Models available include high chests of drawers (for wardrobes, see previous chapter), low-level units and built-in dressing tables that can be installed round corners. They can look very smart and come in a range of styles, materials,

colours and finishes. However, fitted furniture tends to be more expensive than freestanding, though the price is usually inclusive of full design and fitting.

When choosing your bedroom furniture remember that it can be as traditional or as modern as you wish. Apart from pine, which is very popular, you can also find rich mahogany, cherrywood, oak, elm and maple finishes.

Even the newly popular special paint effects like sponging, dragging and rag rolling have found their way into the bedroom ranges. A full range of styles is available going from a classical to a modern look.

Colours can range from traditional white and cream melamine with gold trim for the classical look to soft pastels and bright primary colours for a more modern look.

Style is something you should decide firmly before you buy. Your chosen furniture should reflect not just your personal tastes, but also your lifestyle and the purpose of the room – whether it is to be just for sleeping, or something more as well.

If you are trying to create a feminine and romantic atmosphere then a pretty, turned-leg dressing table and ornate cupboards could fit in. A child's or teenager's room will have to serve more than one purpose and you will need to consider shelves and cupboards for storing toys and books as well as clothes, and a dressing table that doubles as a desk.

For complete flexibility, there are several furniture ranges which you can put together yourself in any combination of components to create cupboards, chest of drawers and cabinets. These come in timber or metal and are generally of a high quality.

But beware when buying self-assembly furniture as the general rule is that you get what you pay for, and bedroom furniture at the very cheapest end of the range may not look quite as good as you hoped, however carefully you put it together. You may well find, too, that it is rather less sturdy in the long run.

DRESSING TABLES

MODERN
Style Low-level drawer units linked by matching top create a neat run.
In use Ideally suited to a modern style room. Useful for children's rooms as it makes a good desk.
Watchpoint You can improvise with filing cabinets and a worktop.

INTEGRATED CORNER
Style Corner-shaped dressing table built into the corner of the room and integrated with a run of other fitted furniture.
In use An excellent space-saver providing both drawers and a surface in an area that is usually wasted. This type of dressing table can also stand alone.
Watchpoints It can be difficult to get sufficient daylight behind the dressing table, so you may have to consider an artificial source of light such as lighted mirror or a wall lamp directly above.

COVER ALL
Style Kidney-shaped dressing table supplied with a rail for a curtain which runs around the dresser to cover its contents.
In use Provides lots of storage space. The curtain keeps all the drawers out of sight.

CLASSIC
Style Classic style freestanding dressing table which normally has a large integral mirror and little drawers or shelves above for jewellery and small items and one or two drawers below for hankies, underwear and other small items.
In use Makes a good focal point in a traditional setting. Usually available in a solid wood.
Watchpoint Like any dressing table, it needs good light behind and is traditionally positioned in front of the window. This style of dressing table can also be rather imposing in a small room and some designs provide little storage for the size (though there are models with drawers next to the knee hole to provide more storage).

BUILT-IN
Style Dressing table area built into a run of floor-to-ceiling cupboards.
In use A very neat option in a fully fitted bedroom. The winged mirrors can be useful for looking at the back of your head. Watch out for some of the special facilities such as slide-out cosmetic trays and spaces large enough to hold bottles for storage.
Watchpoints Because the style is fully fitted giving a more modern look, you may be restricted in style. Artificial lighting is essential as the dresser cannot normally be positioned in front of a window.

CHEST OF DRAWERS

LOW CHEST
Style Long, low horizontal run of drawers of varying sizes.
In use Useful for fitting under a window or along the bottom of the bed. Some models have a combination of small and large drawers – the smaller drawers are handy for socks and hankies.
Watchpoints Always ensure you have sufficient floor space in front to pull out drawers fully.

HIGH CHEST
Style Tall stack of drawers, sometimes with mirror on top.
In use Ideal for flat-storing clothes such as jumpers, underwear and T-shirts.
Watchpoint Because they are narrow they are useful for positioning across awkward corners but ensure that it is not too tall to be used comfortably.

BASKET DRAWERS
Style A rack of open baskets that pull out like drawers in a column of up to five baskets.
In use An inexpensive alternative to a chest of drawers for a high tech or modern bedroom setting, useful for storing shoes and bedlinen.
Watchpoint A practical arrangement but one that is open to dust so possibly not a sensible option in older properties or for untidy people.

BLANKET BOXES

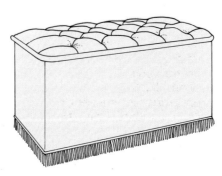

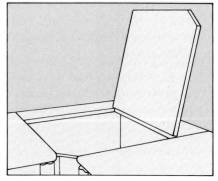

ANTIQUE CHESTS
Style Traditional blanket chest that can be genuine antique or reproduction, plain or panelled, even intricately carved.
In use Good for storing blankets and woollens and usually placed at the bottom of the bed or under the bedroom window. Choose a style to match other bedroom furniture.
Watchpoint If buying antiques, check for woodworm and sturdy construction – stripping often weakens the joints. A cedar chest could be a sensible option to keep moths away.

PADDED BOX
Style Chest with padded lid designed to match other bedroom furniture. Sides are plain painted, stained, or fabric-covered.
In use Positioned at the end of the bed or under the window. This type of box makes a useful seat as well as providing handy storage.
Watchpoint Fixed upholstery may get dirty and need cleaning. The padded top will make the box unsuitable for resting things on.

CORNER BOX
Style Built-in corner box, designed as part of a fitted run of units and making use of corner space that is often wasted.
In use Ideal for storing bedlinen, towels, large jumpers and – in children's rooms – toys.
Watchpoint Only available within fitted ranges unless you improvise yourself with a little woodworking. Make sure it is accessible enough to be able to reach the bottom easily.

BEDSIDE CABINET

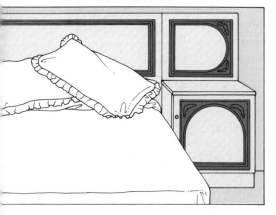

FITTED CABINETS
Style Wall-mounted cabinets (in a large range of styles) either side of the bed and fully integrated with the headboard.
In use A neat way to provide surface space for a bedside lamp, and alarm clock/radio. The space below can be an open storage area or incorporate drawers or a cupboard.
Watchpoint Might be difficult to replace if not changing the whole unit.

TRADITIONAL CABINET
Style Old-fashioned, freestanding pot cabinet with drawer above. Usually varnished timber or painted finish – can be antique or reproduction.
In use Makes a useful bedside cabinet in a traditional style. Handy for storing books, etc.
Watchpoint Because this type of cabinet is freestanding, you must ensure that it is the correct height – neither too tall nor too short to rest a lamp or alarm clock on if necessary.

BEDROOM TROLLEY
Style High-tech metal trolley which can be used in the same way as other bedside cabinets.
In use A flexible bedside facility that can be wheeled to another part of the room if required. Usually supplied with one or two shelves below.
Watchpoint Open style means items are permanently on display. Check height of trolley and make sure it is not too free wheeling – some models have lockable wheels.

INDEX

A

Alarm, baby, 51
Appliqué hanging, 67
Armchair, 48, 49
Art gallery, 61, 65
Attic rooms, 27-32, 44, 75-6, 78

B

Babies, rooms for, 51-6
Barre, ballet practise, 64
Bases, for beds, 85-6
Basket drawers, 94
Bathrooms
    for elderly parents, 81, 84
    for young adults, 77
Bean bags, 71
Bedding, 89-90
    children's, 60
Bedcovers, 39, 46
Bedheads, 44
    built-in storage, 20, 22, 39-41, 72
Bedrooms, perfect, 45-50
Beds, 20, 39-44, 45-9, 85-8
    for children and young people, 59,
        63-8, 71, 72, 76
    for guests, 33-7
    planning, 7
Bedside cabinets, 94
Bedsitting rooms, 75-80
Bedsteads, 88
    antique iron, 46
    brass, 19
Blanket boxes, 21, 22, 34-6, 47, 54,
    78, 94
Blinds, 46, 48, 50
    for attic rooms, 30
    to conceal storage, 14
Bookshelves, 40, 68
Border, wallpaper, mitring, 32
Brass beds, 85, 88
Bunk beds, see Beds

C

Cabinets, bedroom, 94
Cane headboards, 87
Canopy, bed, 64
Chair bed, 34
Chairs, 52, 60, 71
Cherrywood, for furniture, 93
Chests of drawers, 9-14, 46, 47, 53,
    54, 60, 94
Children's rooms
    (0-2), 51-6
    (2-5), 57-62
    (5-12), 63-8
    (12-17), 69-74
    (young adult), 75-80
Clock-radio, 46
Colour schemes
    and space illusion, 4-5
    teenage, 74
    young adult, 80
Computers, space requirements, 71

Conversions, for extra room, 69, 81
Corona, 43, 45, 49
Cots, 51, 52, 55
Cotton fabrics, 90
Cradles, 52
Cupboards
    for children, 63
    overhead, 9, 11
Curtains, 46
    for attic rooms, 29-31
    for babies' rooms, 54

D

Decor
    attic rooms, 27
    children's rooms, 51, 65
    for space illusion, 12-13
    teenagers' rooms, 74
    young adults' rooms, 80
Desks, 19, 49, 69, 70, 71
    child's, 32, 61, 63, 66
Dimmer switches, 15, 54
Divans, 86, 87
    base, co-ordinating, 65
Doors
    bi-fold, 92
    folding, 11, 81, 82
    mirrored, 64
    sliding, 40, 92
Dormer brackets, swivelling, 44
Down fillings, for bedding, 89
Downlighters, 16, 41
Drawers, 93, 94
Dressing tables, 9-13, 23-6, 40, 93
Duvets, 89, 90

E

Elderly parents, accommodation, 81-4
Elm, for furniture, 93
Extension, for elderly parents, 81

F

Fabrics, 39
    bedlinen, 90
    draping and swagging beds, 43-4
Feather fillings, for bedding, 89
Filing cabinets, 78
Floorcovering, for children's rooms,
    51, 58, 61, 72
Flooring, 46
Foam
    bedding, 89
    mattresses, 85
Four-poster beds, 43, 88
Furniture, 10-11, 19-22, 58, 73, 93-4
    fitted, 91-2
    modular, 50
    tubular metal, 66
Futons, 35, 58, 76, 78-9

G

Gas, flame failure device, 82
Granny flat, 81-4
Guest rooms, 33-8

H

Half-tester beds, 43, 44
Handles, new, 47, 49

Handrails, 81, 84
Headboards, 48, 87
Headrests, 87
Heating
    for elderly, 83
    childrens' rooms, 54, 63
Hi-fi equipment, 71, 72, 77
Hobby areas, 72
Hospitality checklist, 38

I

Intercom system, 81

K

Kitchens
    for elderly parents, 81-2
    for young adults, 77, 80

L

Lamp, clamp-on, 17
Light switches, 82
Lighting, 7, 15-18, 73
    for babies, 54
    bedside, 17, 20, 22, 34, 39, 48
    concealed, 45
    dressing tables, 23-5
    swing-arm, 49
    for toddlers, 58
Linen fabrics, 90
Living room, for elderly parents, 83
Locks
    child-proof, 57
    two-way, 84

M

Mahogany, for furniture, 93
Maple, for furniture, 93
Mattresses, 46, 48, 85, 87
Mirrors, 49, 54
    cheval, 49, 91
Mobile, 51, 53
Moses basket, 52

N

Nappy changing facilities, 52, 53
Notice board, 73
Nurseries, 51-6
Nylon fabric, 90

O

Ottoman, see Blanket boxes

P

Paint, lead-free, 57
Panic button, 81
Parents, elderly, accommodation, 81-4
Patchwork quilt, 67
Pictures as focal points, 49
Planning, 7-8
Platform beds, 67, 76
Play areas, 57-62
Pillar beds, 88
Pillowcases, 90
Pillows, 89
Pine, for furniture, 93
Polyester cotton fabric, 90
Polyester fillings, for bedding, 89

Q

Quilts, 44, 45

R

Rails, 46, 79
   spiral, 14
Recliner, for babies, 52
Room dividers, 76, 78

S

Safe, 11
Safety, in children's rooms, 55, 57, 63
Sag bag, 21, 70
Sampler, 47
Screens, 38, 47, 50
Seating, 20
Self-assembly furniture, 93
Sewing machine, adapted
   as dressing table, 26
Sheets, 90
Shelving, 39, 40, 69, 72, 78
Shower, with seat, 84
Sisal floorcovering, for bed
   platform and walls, 40
Sitting room, for elderly parents, 83
Sizes, for beds and bedding, 85, 90
Skirt, for dressing table, 23, 26
Sockets, electrical, covers for, 57
Sofa bed, 34, 36, 83
Soundproofing, 72, 77

Space, and bunk beds, 66
Spare rooms, 33-8
Staircases, and attic bedrooms, 27
Stairs, problem for elderly, 81
Stencils
   on chest of drawers, 47
   for toddlers' rooms, 57
Stool, stable for reaching basin, 62
Storage, 7-14, 19, 21-2, 46, 71, 72
   in attic rooms, 28
   for babies, 51-4
   built-in, around beds, 20, 22
      39-41, 72
   for children, 63-4, 66-8
   dressing tables, 24
   in guest rooms, 36
   for toddlers, 58, 61, 62
   wicker basket, 70
   for young adults, 75, 77, 78-9
Style, 8
Suitcases, storage, 38
Swivel rods, 31, 44

T

Tables, bedside, 19, 20, 21, 40
Taps, lever, 82, 84
Tea maker, 46
Teenagers' rooms, 29, 69-74
Telephone, 46, 81
Toddlers' rooms, 57-62

Tog ratings, 89
Towel rail, antique, 20
Toys, storage, 51, 54, 59, 62, 63, 68
Trolleys, 46, 94
TV, 46, 48

U

Upholstery, for mattresses, 85

V

Valances, 43, 90
Visitors, see Guest rooms

W

Wallcoverings, for toddlers, 58, 61
Wallpaper border, mitring, 32
Walls, painted, 72, 77
Wardrobes, 9-13, 46, 48, 91-2
   for babies, 51, 53, 54
   for children, 64, 66, 67
Washbasin, 36, 38, 47
WC, with grab rails, 84
Windows, for attic rooms, 28
Work light, 18
Working space, in attic rooms, 28-9
Worktop, for toddlers' activities, 62

Z

Z-bed, 88

PHOTOGRAPHIC CREDITS
Front cover Marks and Spencer plc, 1 EWA/Michael Dunne, 2-3 EWA, 4-5 Dorma, 6 EWA/Spike Powell, 9 Schreiber, 10 Habitat, 12 Acmetrak, 14(t) PWA International, 14(b) Stag Meredew ltd, 15 PWA International, 16-17 EWA/Michael Dunne, 17(t) Dorma, 18(t) Dulux paints, 18(b) Dorma, 19 Sharps, 20 PWA International, 21 EWA/Michael Dunne, 22(t) Hulsta, 22(b) Hulsta, 23 EWA/Michael Nicholson, 24 G Plan, 25(l) EWA/Tim Street-Porter, 25(r) Luminance, 26(l) EWA/Michael Nicholson, 26(r) EWA/Jerry Tubby, 27 Arthur Sanderson and Sons, 28 Sharps, 29 Camera Press, 30(t) PWA International, 30(bl) EWA/Di Lewis, 30(br) Curtain Net Advisory Bureau, 31 Textra, 32(t) EWA/Michael Dunne, 32(b) Interior Selection, 33 EWA/Michael Dunne, 34(t) EWA/Michael Dunne, 34(b) EWA/Tim Street-Porter, 35 EWA/Michael Dunne, 36 PWA International, 37(t) EWA/Michael Dunne, 37(b) Bill McLaughlin, 38(t) EWA/Michael Dunne, 38(b) Syndication International, 39 Dorma, 40 Camera Press, 41 EWA/Tim Street-Porter, 42 National Magazine Co/Jan Baldwin, 43 Syndication International, 44(t) EWA/Tom Leighton, 44(b) EWA/Michael Crockett, 45 Skopos, 46-7 National Magazine Co/David Montgomery, 48 National Magazine

Co/Andreas von Einsiedel, 49(t) Jean-Paul Bonhommet, 49(b) Top Knobs, 50(t) Dorma, 50(b) Dulux, 51 Maison de Marie Claire/Scotto/Postic, 52-3 Mothercare, 54 EWA/Jerry Tubby, 56(t) EWA/Michael Nicholson, 56(b) Vymura, 57 EWA/Michael Dunne, 58 EWA/Michael Dunne, 59 Dulux paints, 60(t) EWA/Michael Dunne, 60(b) Coloroll, 61 EWA/Julian Nieman, 62(t) The Picture Library, 62(bl) Vymura, 62(br) Addis, 63 Maison de Marie Claire, 64-5 PWA International, 66(t) Schreiber, 66(b) PWA International, 67 EWA/Michael Nicholson, 68(t) Sleepeezee, 68(bl) PWA International, 68(br) EWA/Jerry Tubby, 69 National Magazine Co/Malcolm Robertson, 70(t) Cover Plus, 70(b) Stacpac, 72(t) Vymura, 72(b) PWA International, 73(t) Perrings, 73(b) EWA/Michael Nicholson, 74(t) EWA/Tom Leighton, 74(b) Crown Paints, 75 Hulsta, 76(t) Jalag, 76-7(b) National Magazine Co/David Brittain, 78(t) Jalag, 78-9 Spur Shelving, 79(t) Jalag, 80 Maison de Marie Claire/Pataut/Hirschmarie, 81 National Magazine Co/John Cook, 82(t) Velux, 82(b) Paul Somers Kitchens, 83 EWA/Michael Dunne, 84 EWA/Clive Helm

Stick your favorite picture here

A special message for you

_____

_____

_____

_____

_____

_____

_____

Goodnight Sweet Violet, child of mine,

Held in my arms you're safe and fine.

I gently place you in your bed.

Lay down your pretty sleepy head.

Violet

You're small, and every day is long.

But sleep my love, and you'll grow strong.

I hope you have amazing dreams,
Of toys, and games, and yummy ice creams.

Goodnight Sweet Violet, now go to sleep,

You need to rest, so please don't weep.

For a loving child I would always pray,
When you were born, it made my day.

Violet

All of your family loves you so,

And that love just grows and grows.

You have so much fun ahead of you,
There's nothing that you cannot do.

So, snuggle up with your stuffed toys,

You have no worries, life is a joy.

Goodnight Sweet Violet, close your eyes,

Don't worry about the hows and whys.

You'll make friends, and laugh and play,
To make the most of every day.

Time goes so fast, and soon you'll grow.

Love life my child, go with the flow.

Throughout your life I'll guide your way,
So from your goals you will not stray.

Goodnight Sweet Violet, sleep my love,

I am always close, like a hand in a glove.

Violet

Listen to all the advice I give,

I will teach you the secret of how to live.

Some days are good, and some days are bad,

But, I hope you are happy more than sad.

A soothing lullaby will help you rest,

For you I want the very best.

Goodnight Sweet Violet, please hear my song,

Morning will come, it will not take long.

Goodnight
Violet

Made in United States
Orlando, FL
04 December 2024

54970652R00024